Confusing Collectibles

A Guide to the Identification
of Contemporary Objects
Revised

by Dorothy Hammond

Wallace-Homestead Book Company
1912 Grand Avenue
Des Moines, Iowa 50305

Revised Edition, 1979
First Printing

ISBN 0-87069-242-9
Library of Congress Catalog
Number 79-63076

Printed in the U.S.A.

Published By

Wallace-Homestead Book Company
1912 Grand Avenue
Des Moines, Iowa 50305

With deepfelt gratitude I dedicate this book to my husband, Robert, for his practical help and moral support, and to our three children—Kurby, Kristy and Kiper—without whose patience, cooperation and understanding during the past year this book would not have been possible.

ACKNOWLEDGMENTS

The author expresses deepest appreciation to the following museums, manufacturers, and individuals who have so generously provided information and photograph illustrations in order to make this revised edition possible.

Thanks are especially due to:

A.A. Importing Co., Inc. of St. Louis, Mo. which manufactures a quality line of faithful reproductions

Stephen S. & Carolyn M. Waligurski, Hurley Patentee Manor, Kingston, N.Y. (lighting)

Jerry Beaumont, Beaumont Heritage Pottery, Portsmouth, N.H.

David Ellinger, Pottstown Pa. (theorem painting)

Lester & Barbara Breininger, Robesonia, Pa. (redware pottery)

Susan Hacker, Light Opera, Retailers of Contemporary Art Glass, San Francisco, Calif.

Marjorie S. Yoder, Morgantown, Pa. (theorem painting)

Will Noad, Burriville, Conn. (wood carving)

Orient & Flume Glass Works, Chico, Calif. (art glass)

Percy L. Perkins, Seabrook, N.H. (decoys)

The Potting Shed, Concord, Mass. (Dedham-type pottery)

Olin & Ruby Fisher, Eldorado, Kans. (photos of Marshall Pottery)

Danial Strawser, Stouchsburg, Pa. (wood carvings)

Claudia Hopf, Stouchsburg, Pa. (scherenschnitte, or scissors cuttings)

Thomas Loose, Dauberville, Pa. (whitesmith)

Dorothy Davis, Yarmouthport, Mass. (paintings on wood)

Phil Kelly, Leacock, Pa. (tinsmith)

Elmer Smith, Bridgwater, Va. (author of *TINWARE, Yesterday & Today*)

J.T. Stauffer, Lititz, Pa. (pewterer)

Sally King, Utexiqual Products, Bristol, R.I. (cast iron banks and toys)

Weaver's Ceramic Mold Company, New Holland, Pa.

A-AMERICA, INC. Seattle, Wash. (reproductions of furniture & accessories)

Conestoga Studios, Lancaster, Pa. (coffee mills)

Joseph Clearman (art glass)

Light Opera Studio's Inc. (glass)

Hurley Patentee Reproductions (lighting)

PHOTO CREDITS: John Huey

CONTENTS

DEFINITIONS

Although the word "antique" is flung about rather loosely by the public at large, it is technically defined by the U. S. tariff code as "any object over 100 years old."

A "reproduction" is a "likeness."

To "reproduce" means to "cause to exist again."

"Adapted" is "to make suitable by adjustment."

"Reissue" is to "issue again."

"Fake" is to "impart a false likeness."

All phases of these definitions are interpreted in the field of antiques, since collecting them seems to have passed out of the category of a mere hobby some time ago. Today, the once fine art of collecting has become a business.

INTRODUCTION

The entire field of crafts everywhere today — textiles, wood, metal, glass, ceramics, and a variety of others — is literally bursting with a new vigor. Galleries and shops that deal with such media are proof that the majority of the reproductions made today are certainly worth collecting — along with many items that are a great departure from the traditional look. The demand for antiques, in addition to the scarcity and prices, has created a small army of extremely talented craftsmen across the country — offering a variety of original and oftentimes regional expressions in all fields. That once narrow view that reproductions were not worth collecting has finally been laid to rest. After all, every antique collected today was new once.

The study of these new objects has many facets, all of which become brighter as our knowledge increases. In every period, collectors have been faced with reproductions, but, as the years destroy the surviving symbols of a generation, those articles that remain become very precious to lovers of nostalgia. Rather than depreciate, their value increases with age — oftentimes very substantially — proving that new items do have a place in every generation. There is absolutely nothing wrong with purchasing a new item or a reproduction, as long as the owner doesn't claim that it is an antique.

The items selected to be included in this revised edition are products of contemporary craftsmen and designers *par excellence.* Fortunately for the collector, most of the craftsmen have signed their wares, and frequently many are dated.

On a limited scale, deceptive objects have posed a threat to collectors since ancient times. Today, from one end of the country to the other, people who collect antiques, those who want to live with antiques, and those who have made it their living selling antiques, are primarily concerned about the acceleration in the mass production and distribution of these wares that have been plaguing American collectors during the last three and a half decades. Actually, we have reached the point where it is almost impossible to discuss antiques without mentioning the word "reproduction."

As the demand for antiques increases, the supply diminishes and prices continue their upward trend. The key reason for the burgeoning interest in antiques is that they have come to be regarded as a hedge against inflation—in some instances by 50 per cent or more a year. The second reason is that many people have rising amounts of disposable income to spend as they choose, and it is being put into antiques, partly because of the snob appeal that goes along with being a collector. It's a chic thing to become—sort of a status symbol. And the third reason is the cultural awareness that has emerged from today's high educational standards and the growing interest in history, arts, crafts and artifacts.

A larger share of the antique business (currently estimated at $600 to $700 million per year) is now being sustained by reproductions. At one time, most manufacturers avoided any involvement with them, but economic reasons eventually forced many to join in the lucrative business. Nowadays, the moment any article in the antique field becomes popular, some manufacturer sets out to make an imitation of it, but the manufacturers and the wholesalers are representing these pieces as reproductions. As long as there is a demand for these objects, manufacturers will make a serious effort to meet it by recreating fine glass, porcelain, silver, furniture, etc., of an earlier period. These new pieces are developing a status of their own, and the finer examples will become the intimate and eloquent souvenirs of our era. They will be highly prized by future collectors for what they actually represent—the art of our time, and are worth collecting for historical reasons.

A great many reproductions have been made honestly, for honest distribution to people who cannot afford genuine old pieces. There is absolutely nothing wrong with buying these new objects—as long as they are acknowledged to be what they are. But there is a great deal wrong with buying reproductions in the belief that they are genuine antiques. Unfortunately, many unscrupulous people have taken this opportunity to pass off these wares as old by removing the labels, abrading the objects to simulate wear, and placing them side-by-side with legitimate antiques with no notation to indicate they are new. This is very confusing for beginning collectors, many of whom depend to a large extent upon the integrity of dealers when making their acquisitions. In addition, reproductions often reach the honest dealer or collector by some roundabout route, and will be accepted—and passed on—as authentic, because they were not aware of their existence. These pieces cause many problems in the field of antiques today, especially if priced comparably with original pieces. Naturally, it is not only irritating to be duped; it can also be extremely expensive.

Most reproductions are recognizable and, in fact, can be easily detected by the person who knows what to look for. Among the features that betray these new objects are price (far below the market), slight variations in size and pattern, weight, the use of decorations and colors that were never used for the originals, and the absence of any signs of natural wear. Even porcelain and glass will show some wear around rims or bases. And the feet of any old piece of furniture show signs of the slow abrasions of time; this is quite different from the deliberate physical distressing done with tools and sandpaper.

Artificial scratches are sometimes put on comparatively new pieces of glass to suggest traces of wear from normal daily use. They can be artificially produced by rubbing the object on cement, or with steel wool, sandpaper, or emery board for example. Scratches and wear marks from normal use appear irregular on the exposed areas, whereas those that are artificially made can be recognized by their uniformity and fresh (clean or frosted) appearance.

This brings us to the interesting meaning of the word "authentic" which, strangely enough, can be correctly applied to both the genuine antique and to the reproduction. Usually, when the word "authentic" is used to describe an antique or aged piece, we immediately think of it as something original, or a genuine specimen. Yet, the design of the reproduction may be thoroughly and faithfully authentic and thereby cause much confusion today.

This mass confusion in the field of antiques might be alleviated if the practice of dating copies or reproductions were adopted. Fortunately, some producers do mark their wares, a very helpful practice, as many new pieces are made today from original molds. However, I know of several instances where a raised mark (Imperial's entwined "I G"), has been ground off. Until legislation of some type makes it mandatory that a permanent mark which cannot be altered indicating age be put on new objects, collectors must learn to live with the problem.

The McKinley Act which, since 1891, has required that the name of the country of origin appear on imports, has helped enormously. Still, thousands of items reach our shores today with only a paper label—and this seldom survives the first owner.

Many collectors take comfort in the knowledge that markings are usually a safe way to establish authenticity, and signed pieces are fetching fantastic prices today. These pieces were marked by the artist or the factory at the time they were made. Unfortunately, but inevitably, the law of supply and demand has also brought about imitations of marks because a signed piece is more valuable and desirable. In fact, forged marks appear frequently. It may be of interest to readers to learn that a mere 50 cents is all that is required, in most instances, to add a counterfeit signature to an unmarked piece—new or old.

To supply the demand for reproductions, reissues, and imitations, shops from one end of the country to the other are selling the latest, the best, and the most wanted pieces now being produced. And, surprisingly enough, the owners of these stores report that their biggest sales are made to antique dealers, many of whom, in turn, sell the merchandise as relics.

So, what's the collector to do?

The obvious answer is to stop being an amateur and get serious, because there will always be a few charlatans who are in the business to fleece you.

Start by deciding which types of antiques appeal to you the most, and select one, two or maybe three types that promise to give you the most enjoyment, as each collector must set his own standards.

Becoming an expert takes a lifetime of scholarship, but you can grow knowledgeable—pleasurably—by devoting all the time you can spare to good reading on the subject, and by accumulating experience. Hundreds of books are available, some general, some dealing with special topics in the antique field. Facts such as the historical background of the style and period of your choice, dates, manufacturing methods, types of wood used, etc., are found in books. So—by all means read whenever you have the opportunity. Many excellent books are available at your public library, and you will be surprised at the large selection of material devoted to the subject. And consider investing in a subscription to an antique trade magazine, which, in addition to excellent articles, carries notices of sales, as well as antique shows. Numerous book companies are listed in these magazines, and constant buying and selling are transacted through their columns. In addition, the advertising columns also provide a fine medium for checking prices.

Haunting antique shops and attending the shows is a good way to get an idea what dealers have to offer and what prices they seek. Most dealers who take pride in their business and reputation can be your best teachers. Here you can actually see and examine authentic pieces that interest you, and recognize their special characteristics.

Antique auctions are fun, but risky, especially the country auctions. If you go just to watch, there is no danger; but if you go to buy, get to the sale early and, before the auction starts, study carefully what is being offered. Just because a piece is sold with many old things does not necessarily indicate that it is old. Here prices will vary according to the crowds the auction attracts, and the selling price will depend solely upon how many of the people present happen to want a particular item, and how much they are willing to pay for it. The collector must guard against being hypnotized into bidding fantastic amounts for things he neither wants nor needs, since a group of acquisitive, auction-loving buyers with money to spend can send prices up to ridiculous levels.

Visit stores that sell reproductions whenever you have an opportunity. Learning to compare the authentic with the spurious teaches collectors to be accurate in judging which is which.

Many American cities—almost all major ones—possess excellent museums, and there are more than 1,500 historic houses and buildings in every part of the country where antiques in particular have been perceptively assembled. Here collectors are able to study original furnishings, and judge their quality.

Serious collectors are often surprised how much they learn as they go. Through books and actual experience they learn to distinguish periods and influences, as well as countries of origin. They learn to look for signs of wear, draw clues to the age of a piece by the way it has been constructed, and to distinguish restoration and repair. And with experience, patience and persistence, collectors eventually develop a sixth sense in judging antiques and, at first glance, a piece is either convincing or questionable. If in doubt, leave it alone.

Finally, the best advice I can give a collector, when shopping for authentic antiques (technically defined by the U. S. tariff code as having been made over 100 years ago), is to deal with only well-recognized dealers with reputations for honesty and reliability. The price will be more than elsewhere, but the collector can expect from the dealer a description of the piece bought, including the date and price, and a guarantee of refund if the object is not exactly as represented.

The attempt to provide, within the compass of a single volume, concise and complete information concerning all reproductions being made today would be impossible. However, I will illustrate hundreds of our confusing collectibles being marketed today, pointing out the differences between the new and the original.

This book has been especially written to help people interested in antiques and collectibles develop the skill, knowledge and perceptive eye that will eliminate their doubts and confusion, and enable them to recognize our confusing collectibles, many of which will survive the changes of time and become heirlooms for generations to come. All antiques, reproductions and contemporary pieces shown were selected personally by the author or authenticated by sources considered reliable.

Chapter I
ART GLASS

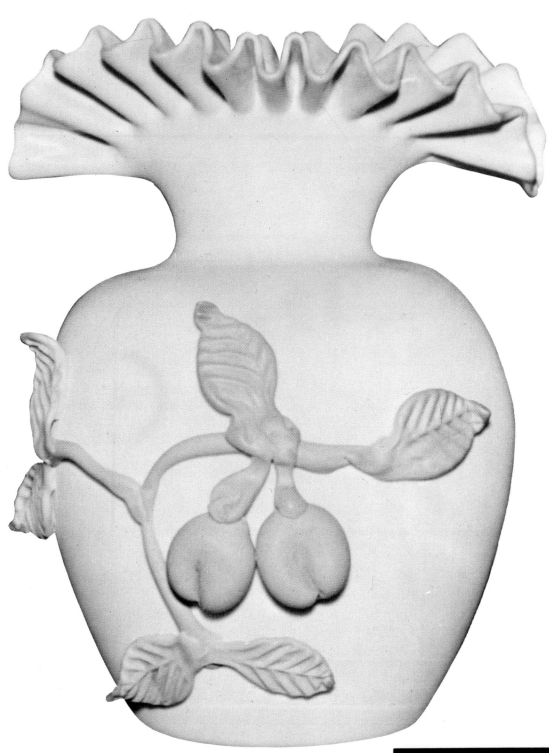

REPRODUCED BURMESE VASE

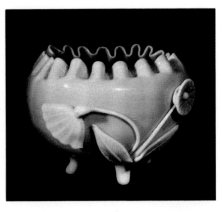

Footed Burmese Bowl
Corning Museum of Glass
Corning, New York

ART GLASS

Art glass is an ornamental glass, made to be decorative rather than functional. It dates primarily from the late-Victorian period to the present day and, during this comparatively short span of time, glassmakers have achieved fantastic effects of color, pattern, shape, texture and decoration.

Practically every type of art glass has appealed to collectors, thus attracting the copyist and creating a sea of confusion in this field. While there are many beautiful and excellent reproductions being made, they are not of the quality and fine craftsmanship made by the early glass blowers.

Fortunately, today's glassmaker prefers to depend upon his own ingenuity to originate new forms, rather than to try the more difficult task of closely imitating the originals. Therefore, the quality of the glass is different, as well as decorations, and only a small number of reproductions have actually been made in an original form. But, strangely enough, the enthusiastic collector acts on impulse, and he only sees what he wants, sometimes missing the characteristics which identify the fake—because these examples seem like only a logical variation, so they are accepted as originals.

The fascination for collecting genuinely fine examples or rarities in this field at this point in time has never been equaled in history. There is still an enormous range of possibilities for new collectors embarking on collecting art glass, but they should choose one specialty and stick to it, reading everything they can find on the subject. Being knowledgeable enables collectors to recognize quality and accumulate a meaningful collection that will grow in value.

Finally, whatever price level a collector decides on, he should start with quality at that level and collect what appeals to him; and never hesitate to ask an expert for advice before making an investment, because prices are too high for speculation by amateurs.

IS IT SIGNED?

This question has been asked many thousands of times in antique shops all over the country and, with interest in art glass remaining high, it will continue to be asked. After constant bombardment with this question, some "enterprising" people have decided to accommodate the paying customer. The processes used by glass manufac-turing firms are not deep, dark secrets known only to a precious few. Anyone with a few evenings to spare can go to the public library and read up on every phase of glass, including manufacturing, decorating, etching and coloring.

The techniques for signing glass are standard and are quite easy to duplicate. The most widely used during the Victorian period and most duplicated today is the hand-inscribed process using a small abrasive wheel. Grinders can be purchased from almost any hardware store for about $20. With one of these units and some practice, anyone with a little dexterity can duplicate the original signatures to almost absolute perfection.

The acid etched signature is probably the one that can fool most people. In some cases it is seemingly buried slightly beneath the surface of the glass and appears impossible to duplicate.

In this particular forging technique an ordinary rubber stamp is made to match the desired signature, a stamp pad is saturated with hydrofluoric acid, the rubber stamp is touched to the pad and then touched to the glass, the exess acid is washed off with water; presto—it's signed. The only discernible difference is in the shape of the lettering within the ribbon. The later signatures have more modern characters. The "S" often has more graceful curves than the original. However, it is only a matter of time before duplicators perfect their stamp, and there will be *no* way to distinguish it from the old. A signature will determine neither the quality, nor the origin of the glass. Thus it becomes more imperative than ever to study the glass, not the signature.

There has been a great deal of glass coming from Europe and then signed in this country. Of this category, one particular group bears mentioning. This is a very pretty shade of cranberry that could be mistaken for Steuben's Cerise Ruby. The pieces are thin and delicate, well blown, usually swirl ribbed, have a belltone ring and applied clear

NEW RUBINA ROSE BOWL WITH
APPLIED FLOWERS

crystal feet and stems on stemware. It is "signed" with the fleur-de-lis and block capital signatures.

Other acid etched signatures being reproduced include Hawkes in block capital letters, Lalique, Webb's Irish Glass, and the modern Webb signature.

Another acid etched technique used during the Victorian period which may show up on today's market is the Stevens & Williams, and Thomas Webb and Sons. In this technique a masking or pellicle is applied in the desired pattern, leaving those areas clean where etching is to occur. The piece is then bathed in hydrofluoric acid, which etches away the field, leaving the characters in relief. Many pieces of English cameo glass have been authentically signed in this manner at the factory. To date, this signature has not been forged to the best of our knowledge.

The "diamond point script" is probably the easiest for the layman to duplicate. Either a sharp piece of diamond or a sharpened and hardened piece of steel is used to scratch the name in the glass. Early pieces of Lalique are known to have been signed by this method, which is still being used by the Lalique firm at the present time. The diamond point script is appearing on all sorts of things today, some correctly marked and some not.

Enameled signatures are quite easy to duplicate; Smith Bros., Lobeyer and Daum Brothers fall into this category. The enamel, when fired on originals, however, shows the telltale signs of microscopic cratering caused by the outgassing. A 10X magnifying glass is usually necessary to see this effect. Rarely will modern forgers take the chance of fracturing their handiwork by firing. In most cases when the enamel has not been fired, a little acetone on a rag will remove the fraudulent work. This is not an infallible test but a good one to keep in mind.

Another technique for applying a signature on glass is the usage of a piece of tape with openings of the correct configuration. When this is applied to the glass, there is a brief blast with the sand blasting machine, and the tape is removed, leaving the signature.

There is a great deal of satisfaction in finding, buying and owning a fine piece of glass produced by gifted artisans. It is truly gratifying to know that the man who made your favorite piece started to work in the glass house, probably at the age of 10, and after many years of apprenticeship finally made the rank of gaffer, entrusted with putting the finishing touches and skill into the creation which resides in your cabinet.

With careful examination and study, learning a little more about this man, it becomes evident that his work need not be signed to carry his trademark. Each glasshouse had its own design and style. Since some were more successful than others, the latter attempted to copy in order to obtain some of the business developed by the successful operators. It is in this area that the sham signatures most often reside, as some still try to ride the coattails of the successful.

The next time you look at a piece of glass and start to ask "Is it signed?" stop and give it a little more thought. Look the piece over carefully; determine what it is, how it was made, who made it and how much it is worth. Then ask the price and decide if you want it or not.

Reprinted from the October 1967 issue of *Western Collector*. Used by permission of J. Weiss, Publisher.

AMBERINA

Amberina was patented by The New England Glass Company in 1883. It is generally recognized as a clear yellow glass, shading to a deep red or fuschia at the top. When the colors are opposite, it is known as reversed amberina. It was machine-pressed into molds, free blown, cut and pattern molded. Amberina has been made by almost every glass company in the United States and Europe, with few pieces being marked. A number of pieces produced by The Libbey Glass Company were marked with the word "Libbey" (acid-etched).

The new amberina ware produced in the United States today looks quite modern and hasn't done any harm, because the new shapes are unlike any known old ones. But the "Flashed Amberina Glassware" that has been reproduced in Italy, Czechoslovakia and other countries during the past few years has caused much confusion. Many dealers, as well as collectors, unsuspectingly bought the new fakes because they were unaware of their existence. The most widely reproduced patterns have been "inverted thumbprint" (sometimes referred to as baby thumbprint, as the depressions are small) and hobnail. A few of the latter pieces (especially water sets and vases) have a satin finish, which is not found on genuine old pieces of amberina.

Flashed wares were popular during the late nineteenth century. They were made by partially coating the inner surface of an object with a thin plating of glass of another, more dominant color

—usually red. These pieces can readily be identified by holding the article to the light and examining the rim, as it will show several layers of glass. Many pieces of "Blue Amberina" (blue to amber), "Rubina Verde" (cranberry to green) and "Rubina Crystal" (cranberry to clear) were manufactured in this way. It should be noted here that Blue Amberina has also been reproduced in the inverted thumbprint pattern.

It is unusual to find a piece of the new "flashed" ware that actually resembles the color of a genuine old piece. The Amberina examples shade from light yellow at the base to a pinkish red at the top, while the Blue Amberina pieces shade from light amber at the base to light blue at the top. One of the most distinct characteristics that identifies practically all of these new pieces is a "+" mold mark on the base. This is especially obvious on the base of a tumbler.

All pieces listed below have been made in the "inverted thumbprint" pattern. An asterick (*) indicates that the piece has also been produced in the hobnail pattern.

Covered Candy Dish
Creamer, 4½" high
Cruet
Finger Bowl or Open Sugar, 4" diam.
Liquor set, 7 pc.
*Pitcher, 9½"
Roemer
*Rose Bowls
Toothpick Holder, crimped edge
*Tumbler

PLATED AMBERINA

Plated Amberina was produced in 1886 by Joseph Locke and was made only for a short time by The New England Glass Company. It is a rare type art glass, considered to be the "queen" of the amberina family. The characteristics that identify this ware are: 1) It shades from a soft golden yellow in the base to a deep fuschia-red at the top; 2) it has a creamy opal lining which almost always has a blue cast; and 3) the most discernible feature is the vertical molded ribs which protrude on the outer layer of the glass.

Collectors should never have any trouble differentiating between the early pieces and the reproductions in this pattern, simply because of their modern shapes and anemic color (note pitcher illustrated). The new examples shade from a creamy white base to a deep orange top, and the opal lining is very good, resembling that of the early ware.

The new pieces that have been made in this pattern are:

Cruet, 7" high
Pitcher, 5", 8" high
Rose Bowl, 3" high
Rose Bowl, Crimped, 5½" high
Tumbler, 4" high
Vase, 3", 12" high
Vase, bottle, 11" high

AVENTURINE

The Venetians are credited with the discovery of Aventurine during the 1860's. It was produced by various mixes of copper in yellow glass. When the finished pieces were broken, ground or crushed, they were used as a decorative material by glassblowers. Therefore, a piece of Aventurine consists of tiny glittering particles on the body of the glass object, suggestive of sprinkled gold crumbs or dust. Other colors in Aventurine may be found.

Collectors will undoubtedly find it difficult to differentiate between the old and the new Aventurine, because the latter is of extremely good quality. However, there is one characteristic that identifies the spurious ware, and that is various small gold colored ovals (verticle), which are scattered over the surface, creating an attractive pattern.

BURMESE GLASS

Frederick Shirley developed this shaded glass at the now famous old Mt. Washington Glass Company in New Bedford, Massachusetts, and patented his discovery under the trade name of "Burmese" on December 15, 1885. The Mt. Washington product was made for a period of five or six years and, though it was never signed or marked, paper labels are known to exist. Burmese was also made in England by Thomas Webb and Sons. Many articles made by Webb were marked, either with a paper label or incised in the glass itself. The registry number 80167 can be found etched or engraved on some pieces.

There are many distinguishing features that aid the collector in identifying Burmese. It is a hand-blown glass with the exception of a few pieces that were pattern molded. These pieces are either ribbed, hobnail, or diamond quilted in design. The pontil mark was often hidden by a "berry-shaped" piece of glass, which was an added means of identification. This ware is found in two textures or finishes, the original glazed or shiny finish and the dull, velvety, satin finish. It is a homogeneous glass (single-layered) that was never lined, cased, or plated. Many pieces are decorated.

The color of Burmese varies slightly, but it always shades from a delicate yellow at the base to a lovely salmon-pink at the top. The blending of colors is so gradual that it is difficult to determine where one color ends and the other begins. When this ware is first removed from the fire, it is an opaque yellow. When the workmen refire it, the sections exposed to the heat turn pink.

Collectors of Burmese should know that the thin yellow line found frequently on the top of some pieces is caused by a second refiring that produces varied effects. In no way does it indicate that the piece is a new one.

The new Burmese ware that has been produced in Italy for approximately six years does not compare with the original ware made in America and England during the late 1800's. The most noticeable variations are in color, shape and weight (heavier). You will note how the new shapes differ from those of the old original pieces. The coloring on the new ware does not always blend well; actually it is often streaked and wavy. Colors shade from a murky yellow to a dull shade of pink, while others shade from a deep rose (purplish cast) to ivory. Many of the latter pieces have confused collectors and dealers as the coloring resembles Gundersen Burmese. This ware was produced around 1952 by the Gundersen-Pairpoint Glass Works of New Bedford, Massachusetts (successors to the Mt. Washington Glass Company and its successor, the Pairpoint Corporation). The company also produced Peach Blow and Rose Amber, and today these wares are highly prized by collectors.

The writer regrets that photos of the above pieces were not available in time for publication.

Other distinguishing characteristics of the new Burmese are the prominent ridges seen on the vases, pitchers, and bowls; the handles on the pitchers differ from the originals; the type of crimping on the edges of vases, pitchers, and bowls was never used on the early pieces; and every new piece of Burmese that I have examined has had a rough pontil, showing two colors mixed together, or a large spot of the deep rose color, varying in size with each piece.

The following list of "new" Burmese pieces does not include FENTON BURMESE (see below).

Basket, 6″ high

Bell, 5½″ high

Bowls in various sizes, some footed, plain and decorated

Compote, open 5¼″ high

Creamers in various sizes

Cruet, 6¼″

Cup and saucer

Duck, 7″ high

Epergne, 9″ high

Ewer, plain and decorated, 9″ high

Fairy lamps, in various sizes, some with Clark base

Fish

Goblet

Jack-in-Pulpit vase

Paperweights, (egg-shaped) 3½″ and 4½″ high

Pitcher, water

Rooster, 7″ high

Rose bowl

Shakers, Salt and Pepper

Sugar bowl

Swan, 6″ high

Toothpick holder

Tumbler

Vases in various sizes, plain and decorated

FENTON BURMESE

One of the greatest steps forward in the field of art glass took place early in 1970, with the re-creation of famous Burmese Glass by an American glass factory. The Fenton Art Glass Company produced six different pieces, available in plain satin or decorated Burmese. The quality of this new ware is excellent, with the homogenous blend of colors appearing consistent on all pieces. And like the "new" Fenton Carnival glass to be marketed this year, Fenton Burmese glass will be marked "FENTON" in raised letters. The new Burmese pieces are: Fairy Lamp, with matching fluted base; Syrup Pitcher; Handled Basket; 7 inch vase with bulbous bottom; Rose Bowl; and an 8 inch gently scalloped bowl.

NEW BURMESE PIECES

VASE

CRUET

GOBLET, 5⅜" tall.

TOOTHPICKS and BASKET

CHEESE DISH, 8¾" across. 2-piece.

JOSEPH CLEARMAN

The new, do-it-yourself phenomenon known variously as "art glass" or "studio glass" these days is strictly American, even though its procedures are being copied in Europe.

The new generation of glass artist-producers include many talented individuals, mostly under the age of forty. Because of the quality of their work, it has been widely exhibited and purchased by many private collectors as well as museums, both here and abroad.

Joseph Clearman's blown glass lamps are considered to be the finest produced today. Because the lamps are blown, it is impossible for any two to be exactly alike. Colors are usually gold and brown — the most popular combination — but on occasion he works with other colors. Presently, Clearman and Lynn Kirshbaum are producing raised and intaglio designs for vases and lamps with matching shades. Together, these young craftsmen are achieving unusual designs by this special process.

All lamps produced by Joe Clearman are signed and dated — on the inside of the base — making them true collectors' items. His lamps are sold by Light Opera Studios, Inc., retailers of contemporary art glass of San Francisco, California. (See photo on following page.)

Art Glass Lamp by Joseph Clearman.
Courtesy: Light Opera Studios, Inc.

"Coralene" Bowl; about 1890, American or English. Fruit or berry bowl of white and pink cased glass with a diamond pattern air trap between and with applied tiny glass beads in a coral pattern. H. App. 4¼". Courtesy of Corning Glass Center.

CORALENE

The name Coralene is a type of decoration, rather than a kind of glass, consisting of many tiny beads, either of colored or transparent glass. Usually the decoration was applied to an acid-finished piece with an adhesive, to which were stuck thousands of beads and these were secured by firing. The most popular design used resembled coral or seaweed, hence the name Coralene.

Unfortunately for the unsuspecting collector, many pieces of genuine art glass have appeared on the market with newly applied coralene decoration. The glass beads being used for this fakery are the kind used in reflective road markings. These newly-decorated pieces may appear genuine, but can be easily detected if touched. Since the glass beads do not adhere to the adhesive agent used, they fall off quite easily when touched.

CRACKLE GLASS PITCHER

Reproduced square mouth water pitchers are rare. This beautiful example will confuse many collectors because of its shape and applied clear glass handle. Courtesy of the Pilgrim Glass Corp.

CRACKLE GLASS

Crackle glassware dates from the sixteenth century. It was an invention of the Venetians that spread rapidly to craftsmen in other countries.

This ware is produced by plunging red-hot glass into cold water, then reheating and reblowing it—thus producing an unusual outer surface which appears to be covered with a multitude of tiny fractures. The interior surface is perfectly smooth.

The Pilgrim Glass Corporation of Ceredo, West Virginia, has reproduced many fine pieces of this ware, mostly in contemporary forms. The pitcher illustrated will confuse many collectors because its shape is like many of the early pitchers produced during the latter part of the nineteenth century. This new Crackle glass can be easily detected, however, since its quality is not comparable to the early ware. An example of the latter has so many fractures on its surface that, from a distance, the piece will have a frosted appearance, whereas the crackle effect on a new piece will only appear wavy from a distance.

CRANBERRY GLASS

The term "Cranberry Glass" refers to color only, not to a particular type of glass. It is undoubtedly the most familiar colored glass known to collectors and, because of its popularity, numerous pieces have been reproduced, many in the "thumbprint" pattern. The color and weight of the early reproductions is quite different from those of the nineteenth century pieces. The ware is thicker than the original, thus causing these spurious examples to be heavy, and many of the "new" pieces have a purplish cast. The color has improved, however, but not the weight, as many pieces being produced in Japan, as well as the United States, remain quite thick.

The quality of the new Cranberry pieces being made today by The Pilgrim Glass Corporation of Ceredo, West Virginia, is very good and the color is excellent. However, their contemporary shapes date them; therefore, I don't feel that the Pilgrim ware will cause much confusion among collectors.

THESE ARE ALL "NEW" CRANBERRY PIECES
Courtesy of the Pilgrim Glass Corp.

Vase

Bowl

Stemmed Vase

Urn

Carafe

A group of 7" Cranberry Vases. Similar vases may also be found in Blue, Green, Light Amber and Tangerine.
Courtesy of the Pilgrim Glass Corp.

MORE NEW CRANBERRY PIECES

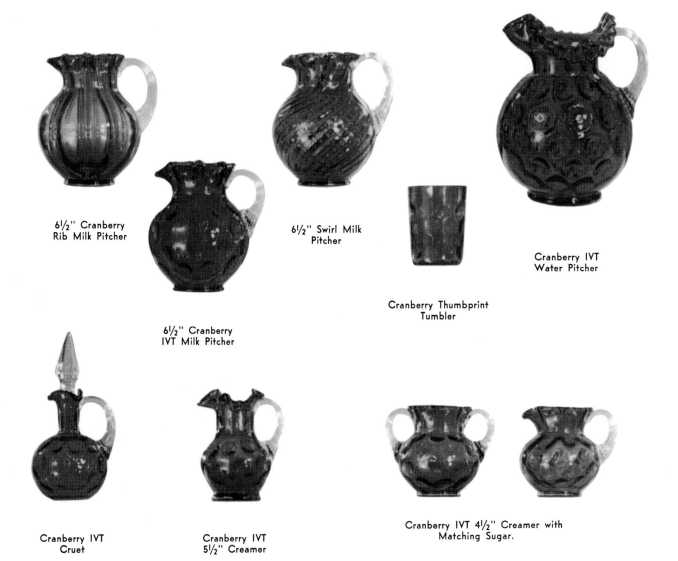

6½" Cranberry
Rib Milk Pitcher

6½" Swirl Milk
Pitcher

Cranberry IVT
Water Pitcher

6½" Cranberry
IVT Milk Pitcher

Cranberry Thumbprint
Tumbler

Cranberry IVT
Cruet

Cranberry IVT
5½" Creamer

Cranberry IVT 4½" Creamer with
Matching Sugar.

FRENCH CAMEO GLASS

Although Cameo Glass has been made over a span of centuries, most pieces collected today date from the mid-nineteenth century. It can be defined as any glass in which the surface has been cut away to leave a design in relief, and the cutting can be accomplished by the use of hand cutting tools, wheel cutting and hydrofluoric acid. Cameo Glass can be clear or colored glass of a single layer, or glass with multiple layers of clear or colored glass.

Cameo Glass was made in England, as well as France, and other parts of Europe. It was also produced in the United States by the Boston and Sandwich Glass Company, the Mt. Washington Glass Company and others, but none of the American cameo ware was considered to be quality glass.

The French technique of acid-engraving cameo relief designs on glass became popular in France about 1890, and production continued well into the twentieth century. The most famous of the French masters of Cameo Glass was Emile Galle. Although French Cameo Glass is still rather abundant, it has become very collectible and the steadily rising prices for the finer examples show no signs of abating. So—imitations and reproductions have been produced to supply the demand.

About three years ago an experimental group of signed "Galle" bowls were made, but these pieces proved to be too costly to sell to the masses, so the line was dropped. To be profitable, the distribution of reproductions necessarily depends upon a wide popular demand.

The next discernible pieces of French Cameo Glass to make an appearance were "Le Gras" vases in two sizes. The smaller size is usually signed "Le Gras" in script. The quality of these vases is exceedingly poor and easily recognized by anyone familiar with authentic Le Gras examples, because the background on these scenic pieces is nothing more than a decal and the foreground is several layers of rough textured paint, which has apparently been sprayed on the surface.

In addition to the known types mentioned, there are numerous pieces of glassware being made today that are being sold as a "Cameo" type. The "Le Mans" vase and small rose bowl illustrated are two of the most popular examples being marketed.

Left: Reproduced "LeGras" Vase.
Right: An original "LeGras" Vase, signed.

August J. F. LeGras worked in glass at Saint-Denis near Paris from 1864 until about 1914. He produced a variety of multi-layered, well-cut glass—which can be classified as "French Cameo Glass."

Another "French Cameo Type" vase, signed "Le-Mans" in gold script on bottom. Origin unknown. This piece has a dull satin finish resembling camphor glass. The decoration is enameled flowers, trimmed with gold in relief.

Rose Bowl, product of Japan. This attractive piece (bright blue with white casing) has quality—and was sold as a "cameo type" glass. However, its scenic design in relief was pattern-molded, not cut or etched into its glossy surface.

CORALAY CLASSICS

The most outstanding cameo type work being done today is that which has been produced by Regal Reproductions in Los Angeles. This line is called Coralay Classics and is made up of nineteen pieces. The relief details on every piece has been so lavishly executed, that they almost look as if a slight touch would detach them from the surface.

All Coralay pieces listed and illustrated are available in the following stones: Sardonyx, (brown and white); Onyx, black with white; Green Marble, green and white; and Pink Marble, pink and white.

The other Coralay pieces are:

Alexander the Great, 27"x23"

Tempus, 19"x15"
Merchant of Venice, 23"x17"
Athena, 21½" Diam.
Helen of Troy, 19" Diam.
Artemis, 18½" Diam.
Bacchanalia, 23"x13"
Saint George, 18"x13"
Lovers, 16½"x13"
Retriever with Pheasant, 13¼"x11¼"
Retriever with Hare, 13¼"x11½"
Hercules, 10" Diam.
Ceres and Persephone, 8½" Diam.
Faunus, 7¼" Diam.

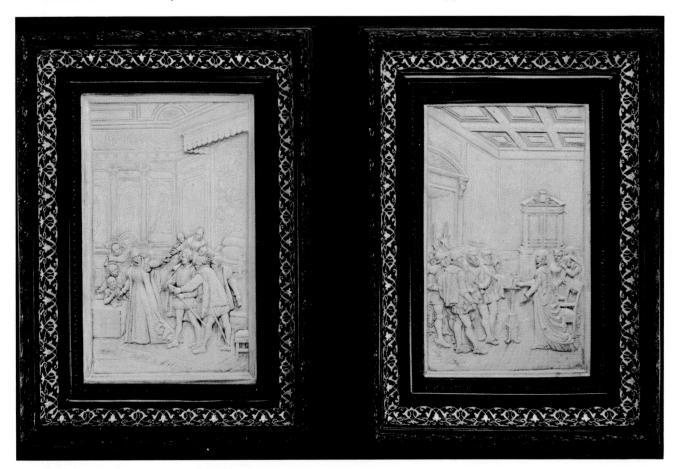

ELIZABETH THE FIRST and MARY-QUEEN OF SCOTS

From an original pair in carved ivory with elaborate ebony frames. An unknown artist carved these delicate panels in Germany circa 1830, undoubtedly a commission from an English noble.

The panels depict Queen Elizabeth ordering the death decree of her rival cousin, Mary, from St. James Palace in London. Mary, at Holyrood Palace in Edinburgh, receives the order that she is to be beheaded.

The original made in an artistic blend of Silver, Bronze, and Gold. The design is attributed to Albert Wilms, and the piece was published by Elkington & Co. in London, Circa 1870.

A REGAL REPRODUCTION

GODDESS OF THE SUN

Original in Silver and Bronze
Created by C. B. Birch
For Hancock's of London
In 1855

The Goddess Aurora (Called Eos by the Greeks)—daughter of Hyperion and Thia—
was well known to Ovid. In his Metamorphoses he writes, "See how Aurora shines and
shadows vanish;", a comment befitting the radiance of the piece.

A REGAL REPRODUCTION

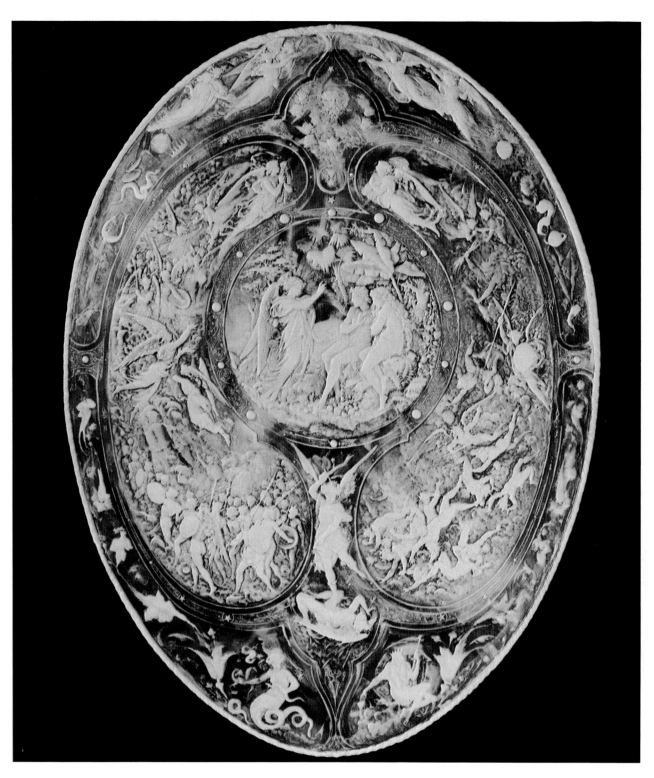

THE MILTON SHIELD

From an original designed and made by L. Morel Ladeuil for Elkington & Co.—
Created in silver and damascened iron in 1866 (Inspired by John Milton's epic poem
"Paradise Lost")

A REGAL REPRODUCTION
Courtesy of Corbell Imports, Los Angeles, California.

25

HOBNAIL

Although a variety of hobnail imitations have been made for years, I have never seen a reproduction that even compares to an original example. Strangely enough, the old technique in making this particular pattern has changed through the years—in addition to shapes—making it easy for collectors to identify the spurious pieces.

The characteristics which identify a genuinely old piece of hobnail are:

1. Hobs are more uniform in size; they are more round than oval and are spaced closer together.

2. It is quite unusual to find an authentic piece of early hobnail that does not have a solid hob, causing these pieces to be heavier than later ones. When the interior of an old piece is examined (pitchers are ideal for this test) closely, you can see as well as feel that the surface where the hob projects will be slightly rounded.

3. The base of any early piece of hobnail will show signs of wear. Hob points will be more rounded in this area, many are chipped or nicked, and the surface of the glass will appear dull, since the gloss has been worn away.

4. This is not an infallible test, but most early pieces have perfectly smooth, round pontils.

New hobnail pieces can easily be distinguished for the following reasons:

1. The rows of hobs are spaced too far apart. Hobs are usually hollow, distorted, blunt and more oval than round.

2. New pieces are not as thick as early examples, and lightweight.

3. The pontil marks are either very rough, sunken or, if ground, the area will be misshapen (usually oval), not perfectly rounded.

It is very difficult to find an original piece of old hobnail in perfect condition, as many of the early examples had hard usage. Frequently, hobs were bumped, causing chips or causing a hob to be completely broken off. So, one of the new tricks of the trade is to make a new hob, which will increase the value of the damaged piece. This is done with clear glue, and the new hob will have a frosted or fractured (many tiny lines caused from each application of the glue) appearance. So, examine old hobnail pieces very closely before buying, because what may appear to be only a bruised hob could be nothing more than a cleverly shaped glob of "glue."

Finally, for the benefit of new collectors, I have illustrated several pieces of authentic old hobnail. Please note the shapes of the hobs on these pieces.

Original Rubena Verde
Hobnail Water Pitcher

Original Cranberry
Opalescent Hobnail
Barber Bottle, Milk Pitcher, Cruet

Original Rubena Verde Opalescent
Hobnail Water Pitcher

NEW HOBNAIL

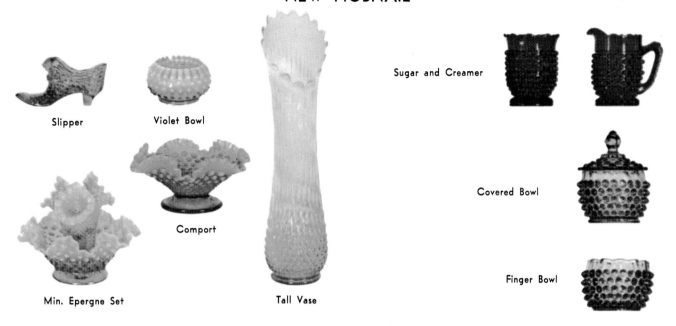

Slipper

Violet Bowl

Comport

Min. Epergne Set

Tall Vase

Sugar and Creamer

Covered Bowl

Finger Bowl

Courtesy of Fenton Art Glass Company

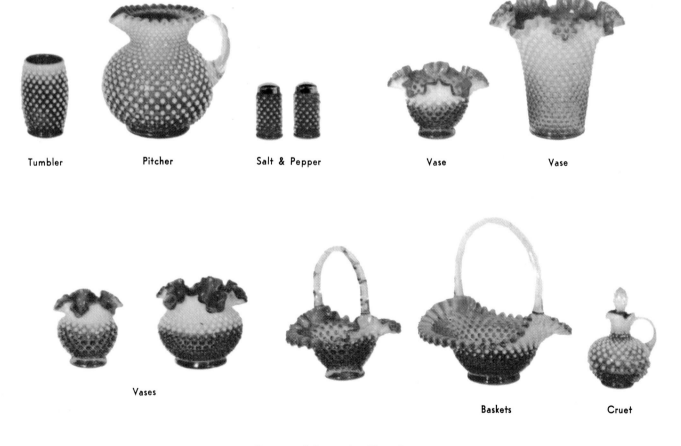

Tumbler

Pitcher

Salt & Pepper

Vase

Vase

Vases

Baskets

Cruet

Courtesy of Fenton Art Glass Company

Reproduced Holly Amber
Toothpick Holder.

Reproduced Caramel Slag
Tumbler in the "Holly"
Pattern.

HOLLY AMBER

Holly Amber glass is very rare and expensive. This molded ware, with its glossy finish and opalescent to amber-colored shadings, was originally called Golden Agate. It was produced by the Indiana Tumbler and Goblet Company for only six months, from January 1, 1903, to June 13, 1903.

The only Holly Amber reproduction known to me at this writing is a toothpick holder. Tumblers have been produced in this pattern, but they can only be classified as poor examples of Caramel Slag glass (see illustration).

The reproduced toothpick holders are easily identified, as they show practically no opalescence and the glass resembles caramel slag, except for the holly band which is the color of Vaseline glass. An authentic Holly Amber toothpick will have an amber band, frequently showing some opalescence.

Like the hobnail pattern, occasionally a piece of Holly Amber can be found that has one or several new beads made from clear glue. A fake opalescent bead is easily detected, but a stained amber one is more difficult to spot. A magnifying glass is quite helpful in detecting these spurious new beads.

Butter dish in "Holly Amber" or "Golden Agate" glass. Made by the Indiana Tumbler and Goblet Company, Greentown, Indiana, between January and June 1903.

28

LATTICINO

"Latticino" is the name given to articles of glass in which a network of milk-white lines appear, crisscrossing between two walls of glass. It is a type of Filigree glassware developed during the sixteenth century by the Venetians.

Latticino glassware is being produced today on the small island of Murano, only a short distance from Venice. The new examples exhibit a network of milk-white threads, in addition to colorful vertical stripes on a crystal ground. These pieces are sometimes called "Venetian" or "Ribbon Glass."

The New Latticino pieces are:
  Bell, 5"

Bird, 6"
Box, Round, Hinged, 6"
Cruet, 8"
Cup and Saucer
Duck, 6½"
Fish, 7"
Pitcher, 9"
Plate, 4" square
Sugar and Creamer, 2½"
Swan, 6½"
Toothpick Holder
Tumbler, 4¼"
Vase, 7"

"NEW" LATTICINO GLASS

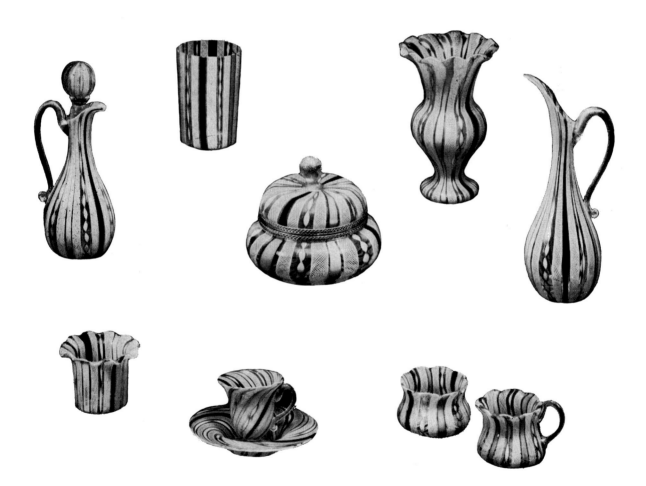

MAIZE

W. L. Libbey & Son's "Maize" pattern was designed by Joseph Locke and was offered to the public in 1889. The ware was produced in opaque white, ivory, and a pale celadon green glass. It is a mold-blown glassware, intended to look like kernels of corn with corn leaves in color (blue, green and brown), which fan out at the base. Occasionally the detail of the leaves is picked out in gold.

The new "Maize" pattern produced today by the L. G. Wright Glass Company is obviously an adaptation of the earlier ware. It is easily identified as the ware is cased, many pieces with contrasting colors. Only two of the new pieces resemble the original forms, and these are tumblers and sugar shakers, with a thin white lining. I have seen other pieces of this ware that has a thick chalky white lining. The new Maize glass is produced in shades of pink, rose, white, yellow (listed as amber in catalogues), light and dark blue, with leaves of the same color.

The following articles have been produced in the "new" Maize pattern:

Covered Candy Dish
Lamps, in various shapes
Pickle Jar
Pitcher, water
Rose Bowl
Shakers, salt and pepper
Sugar Shaker
Tumbler
Vases

NEW MAIZE PIECES

Maize pattern
Pickle Jar in
Silver Frame with Tongs.

Maize pattern Rose Bowl

Maize pattern
Water Pitcher and Tumbler

Maize pattern
9" Vase

Maize pattern
7" Vase

REPRODUCTIONS
Row 1: "Bennett" New England
Peachblow Pitcher and Vase
Row 2: Burmese Rosebowl; Mt.
Washington Peachblow Fairy
Lamp
Row 3: Wheeling Peachblow Tooth-
pick; Burmese Basket;
"Bennett" Water Pitcher

31

MARY GREGORY

Mary Gregory was an artist for the Boston and Sandwich Glass Company, Sandwich, Massachusetts, during the 1870's or 1880's. She painted white enamel figures of young children, engaged in collecting butterflies always in white on transparent glass, both clear and colored. The term "Mary Gregory" glass applies to any glassware that remotely resembles her work. Many European examples have been produced through the years; and quantities of reproductions have been marketed. Therefore, much of the ware has been erroneously attributed to the Sandwich factory. The authenticity of a piece of this glass should be determined by an expert.

The Mary Gregory pieces on the market today lack the quality and finished detail of the complete subject, including the children's facial features, and the enameling on the new ware chips easily.

A group of Mary Gregory Type Vases on Black Glass and Blue Glass with a Satin Finish. Courtesy of the Westmoreland Glass Co.

NEW MARY GREGORY
handpainted white enamel figures on cranberry glass

Early "Mary Gregory" Barber Bottle

"Mary Gregory" Barber Bottle

Courtesy of the Henry Ford Museum, Dearborn, Michigan.

33

NEW MARY GREGORY PIECES THAT HAVE BEEN PRODUCED

CRYSTAL

Bell
Bottle
Box
Cruet
Pitcher
Sugar/Creamer
Tumbler
Vase, 6″, 8″

AMETHYST

Bottle, Perfume
Box, 4″
Box, Candy, 6″
Cachepot, 5″
Cigarette set, 2 pc.
Cruet, 5″
Jar, Apothecary, 9″
Tumbler, 4″
Vase, 5″, 6″

BLUE OPALINE

Bottle, Perfume
Cachepot, 8½″
Cigarette Set, 2 pc.
Cruet
Jar, Apothecary, 7½″, 9½″
Tumbler
Vase, 5½″, 8½″

AMBER AND RUBY RED

Bottle, Perfume, 6½″
Box, Candy
Box, Powder, 4½″
Cachepot
Cigarette Set, 2 pc., 4″
Cruet, 5⅜″ Tall
Goblet, 7¼″
Goblet, Wedding, 7⅞″
Jar, Cotton, 6¼″
Vase, 5″, 5½″, 8¼″
Vase, Flip, 5½″, 7″
Vase, Goblet, 5½″

CRANBERRY

Bell, 6″ tall
Bottle, 9½″ tall
Bottle, Perfume, 6¼″ tall
Box, 6″ diam.
Box, Powder, 4″, 4½″

Cachepot, 5″
Candleholder, 10″, 12″
Cigarette set, 2 pc.
Compote, Crimped, 9″
Cruet
Cruet, 5⅜″ tall
Cup/saucer
Dresser set, 3 pc.
Goblet, 7½″ tall
Jar, Apothecary, 9″, 10″, 12″
Jar, Cotton, 6¼″
Mug, applied handle
Night set, 3 pc.
Pitcher, 9½″ tall
Roemer
Sugar/Creamer
Tumbler, 3½″, 4″ tall
Vase
Vase, 5″, 6″, 8″, 8¼″, 10″ tall
Vase, Crimped, 10″

COBALT BLUE

Bell, 6″ tall
Bottle
Box, 6″ diam.
Cruet, 6″ tall
Dresser
Jar, Apothecary
Mugs
Night set, 2 pc.
Pitcher
Sugar/Creamer set
Tumbler
Vase, 6″, 8″ tall

GREEN

Bell, 6″
Bottle, 9½″
Box, 6″ diam.
Candleholder, 10″, 12″
Cruet, 6″
Cup/Saucer
Dresser set, 3 pc.
Jar, Apothecary, 12″
Mug
Night set, 2 pc.
Pitcher
Roemer
Sugar/Creamer
Tumbler, 3½″
Vase, 6″, 8″, 10″
Vase, Crimped, 10″

MILLEFIORI

Millefiori is considered to be a specialty of the Venetians. It is sometimes called "glass of a thousand flowers," and has been made for centuries, and is still being produced. Very thin colored glass rods are arranged in bundles, then fused together with heat. When the piece of glass is sliced across, it has a design like that of many small flowers. These tiny wafer thin slices are then embedded in larger masses of glass, enlarged and shaped.

The modern Millefiori being produced in Italy is thick and heavier than earlier examples. The design is not sharp or distinct. The coloring is poor and frequently runs together producing a blurred effect because the canes have not been cut smoothly.

The new pieces of Millefiori causing the greatest confusion among collectors are:

Basket, 6″ diam.
Bowl, fluted, 5″ diam.
Cruets
Epergne, 3 arms
Ewer, 9½″ high
Fairy lamp
Hinged Box, 6″ diam.
Paperweights, 3″ and 2″ diam.
Pitcher, covered (or Coffee Pot)
Rose Bowls
Sugar and Creamer, 2″x2¾″ high
Toothpick Holder
Tumbler, water, 4″ high
Vases, 6″ high and 3½″ high

NEW MILLEFIORI GLASS MADE IN MURANO, ITALY

NAILSEA

Nailsea glass was produced in England during the 18th and 19th centuries. The characteristics that identify this glass is the "pulled" loopings and swirls of colored glass over the body of the object, combined with clear or opal glass. This technique has also been used by glassblowers in Italy, France, Germany and the United States.

The new pieces of Nailsea glassware are thicker and heavier than the early examples. And many of these examples have a dull satin finish.

The reproduced pieces are:

Bell, 5″ high
Cruets
Pitchers, 5″ high and 8″ high
Rose Bowl
Tumbler
Vase

CUT OVERLAY

Although Bohemian glass manufacturers produced some very choice pieces of Cut Overlay during the nineteenth century, fine examples were also made in France, England and America. A variety of reproduced Cut Overlay glassware has been imported during recent years, and the quality is quite good. Most pieces have milk-white exteriors that have been cased with cranberry, blue or amber glass. Other examples are deep blue, amber or cranberry, on crystal glass, and the majority of pieces have been decorated with dainty flowers. The lack of normal wear marks and a "slick" surface identifies most pieces. As far as it is known, there has never been any triple cased cut overlay produced; however, many new pieces have been decorated with gold, to simulate a three-layered effect.

"NEW" NAILSEA TYPE
Two handled vase, 6¾″ tall, footed. White loops on blue or cherry background. Made in satin or glossy finish. New cruets have also been made in this pattern.

**NEW CUT OVERLAY GLASS
WHITE CUT TO CRANBERRY**

"NEW" NAILSEA GLASS
Available with red loops on white satin glass, or with blue loops on white.

36

ORIENT & FLUME GLASS WORKS

Another firm doing great things in the field is Orient & Flume Glass Works of Chico, California. It is regarded as the largest iridescent glass factory in the country. Seventeen youthful artisans are now affiliated with the firm. David Hopper, co-owner of Orient & Flume Glass Works, attributes the success of the business to choice of art nouveau design style so popular around the turn of the century, along with the superior quality of their products.

Art glass made by Orient & Flume is well marked (see illustration of mark). The registration number is in numerical order of the date made. For example, the mark shown here would indicate the twenty-first of April, 1978. There is a different sequence of numbers and letters for each type of glass produced, whether it be a miniature, paperweight, vase, lamp, jewelry, egg, or stained glass box. For future identification, the registration number can be generally correlated for the records of the types of glasses, colors, and shapes or pattern, as new ones are developed. All products are marketed exclusively with N.S. Gustin Company of Los Angeles.

Orient & Flume Trademark.

Contemporary Art Glass Pieces by Orient & Flume Glass Works.

37

NEW CUT OVERLAY PIECES
(amber or cranberry over white)
Made in Czechoslovakia.

Bohemia: c1840. Triple Cased, Footed
compote, blue over white over crystal

PEACHBLOW GLASSWARE

Peachblow glassware, with its simple lines and delicate shadings, was produced during the late nineteenth century. The types most commonly encountered are Wheeling, Mt. Washington and New England Peachblow.

The Wheeling type was produced soon after 1883 by J. H. Hobbs, Brockunier & Company at Wheeling, West Virginia. It is a two-layered glass, lined or cased inside with an opaque, milk-white type of plated glassware. The outer layer shades from a bright yellow at the bottom to a mahogany red at top. The majority of pieces found are in the glossy finish.

Mt. Washington Peachblow is a solid glass, being the same composition inside and out. It shades from a delicate rose-pink at the top to a light blue-grey at the base. This ware was produced between 1886 and 1888 at the Mt. Washington Glass Company in New Bedford, Massachusetts. Practically all examples have a soft satin finish.

The New England Peachblow was patented in 1886 by the famous New England Glass Company of Cambridge, Massachusetts. It is a single-layered glass, shading from opaque white at the base to deep rose-red or raspberry at top. Some pieces have a glossy surface, but most were given an acid bath to produce a soft, matte finish.

A more recent type of Peachblow is known as "Gundersen," which was produced in 1952 by the Gundersen-Pairpoint Glass Works of New Bedford, Massachusetts (successors to the Mt. Washington Glass Company and its successor, the Pairpoint Corporation). Gundersen pieces have a soft satin finish, shading from white at the base to a deep rose at the top. The ware is heavier and thicker than earlier types, and the pontil marks are usually large and glossy.

Innumerable new pieces of Peachblow glassware have emerged in this decade, as well as a variety of new types, via experimentation, many of which are a radical departure from the best-known Peachblow colors. New types which have been produced by the Pilgrim Glass Company, Imperial Glass Corp., and The L. G. Wright Glass Company (with Moss Rose decoration) are very colorful and eye-catching, and the quality is superior to the "new" Italian type which has surface decoration (berries and leaves).

The majority of Peachblow reproductions plaguing collectors and dealers today are of Italian origin, and the chief characteristics that identify these pieces are shape, color, weight, thickness, poor crimping on vases and pitchers, in addition to rough pontil marks on all pieces. These spurious pieces can be found in both satin and glossy finish.

The spurious Mt. Washington pieces shade from a murky rose-purple at the top to a bluish-gray color at the bottom. The New England reproductions shade from dark rose to white at the bottom.

The only Wheeling Peachblow reproductions I have examined are toothpick holders (illustrated). These are excellent examples. They shade from mahogany red at the top to ivory at base, and the thin milk-white lining looks right. When these pieces were closely examined, yellow paint was discovered in and around the rough pontil scar. A few drops of turpentine and a small piece of cotton revealed that yellow oil base paint had been rubbed into the surface (ivory color) on both pieces, thus staining the glass just enough to resemble the earlier ware.

In view of the fact that several different types of Peachblow glassware are being produced today, few collectors or dealers were surprised to learn that an original type had been made domestically during the winter months. Approximately 100 pieces (some are illustrated) of New England Peachblow were made from the original formula at The Guernsey Glass Company, Cambridge, Ohio, by Harold Bennett. Production began in November, 1968, and lasted for only a short time; however, Mr. Bennett plans to resume production late in 1969. For easy identification, the Bennett Peachblow pieces are signed in script on the base "BENNETT" (scratched into the glass). When the name is removed, these pieces will become another challenge for the already-confused collectors, since many examples do closely resemble nineteenth-century versions, both in shape and color. However, the ware is thicker and heavier, which seems to be a characteristic of all reproduced Peachblow, with the execption of the new Wheeling examples.

The following reproductions have been produced in New England and Mt. Washington Peachblow (BENNETT PIECES NOT INCLUDED).

Candle Holder
Compote (tall)
Creamers
Cruet
Cup and Saucer
Ewer
Fairy Lamp
Goblet

Rose Bowl (berry pontil, amber applied flowers)
Sugar Bowls (with or without handles, and one of the latter examples has a berry pontil on side)
Toothpick Holder
Vases in various sizes

Basket, 7½" High
Bell, 5" High
Bowl, Handled, 5½" High x 7½" Wide
Bowl, 6" High x 9½"
Chalice, 6½" High
Cruet, 9" High
Decanter, 11" High
Epergne, 16" High
Ewer, 10" High, Handled
Pitcher, 9" High
Rose Bowl, 4½" High
Tray, Footed
Tumbler, 4¾" High
Vase, Handled, 11" High

NEW "DECORATED" PEACHBLOW

Cranberry top shading to blue at bottom. Each piece has berries that are applied in dark blue with leaves, feet, handles and trim in amber. Most pieces have crimped edges and all except the epergne, bell and tumbler have scroll-type feet.

New "Peachblow" Glass made by Imperial Glass Corp., Bellaire, Ohio. (These discontinued pieces have become very collectible — photo from 1968 catalog).

9½" Vase   10½" Vase   7¾" Vase   10½" Vase   Decanter and Stopper

NEW DECORATED PEACHBLOW PIECES

"New" Satin Glass Vase (referred to as "Peachblow", but does not resemble any known early type), with applied leaves and fruit. The inferior quality of the workmanship is plainly apparent, as the berries on this piece are almost flat and poorly shaped.

Top view of vase, bearing obvious tool marks.

NEW PEACHBLOW MINIATURES
Made by The Pilgrim Glass Corp.

MORE COLORFUL "NEW" PIECES OF PEACHBLOW
WITH MOSS ROSE DECORATION
By L. G. Wright Glass Company

Cruet   Pitcher

Pickle Jar

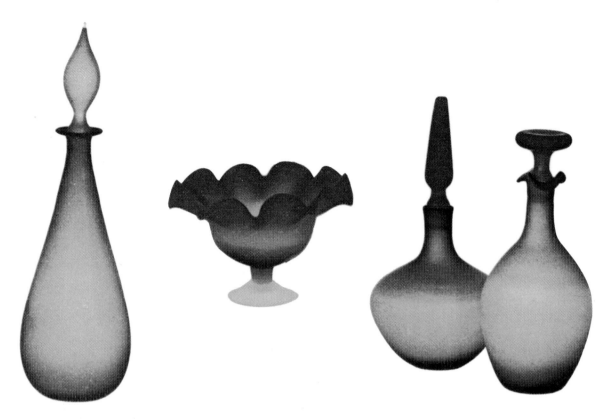

PEACHBLOW DECANTERS AND BOWL made by the Pilgrim Glass Corp., Ceredo, West Virginia. The color of these new pieces combines a blending of Tangerine and Avacado Green in a satin finish (from 1969 catalog).

New Peachblow Pitcher and Tumblers. Moss Rose Decoration, by L. G. Wright Glass Company.

Reproduced Wheeling Peachblow Toothpick Holders, in glossy (left) and satin finish (right).

Editor's Note:

The following information became available too late to be included in the text.

Tumblers and small creamers have also been produced, and like the toothpicks, have rough pontil scars. These new pieces were made in Italy.

Contemporary New England Peachblow, produced in 1968 by Harold Bennett,
Guernsey Glass Co. Inc., Cambridge, Ohio.

PELOTON

Peloton glass is a novel type of art glass ware which originated in Bohemia. It was patented on October 25, 1880, by Wilhelm Kralik. The ware normally has a transparent colored or clear body, with small threads of glass of the same color or numerous contrasting colors scattered over its surface. Many pieces have a satin finish.

The new Peloton vases and small pitchers being marketed today have a clear body, with a variety of multi-colored glass threads. These pieces are extremely attractive; however, they should not confuse the careful buyer, as the glass is thick and weighty. In addition, the new pieces have rough pontil scars. It is extremely unfortunate that not an example is available for illustration.

SATIN GLASS or
MOTHER-OF-PEARL GLASS

Satin glass was produced in this country during the late 1800's by the Phoenix Glass Company in Beaver, Pennsylvania, and by the Mt. Washington Glass Company, New Bedford, Massachusetts. Since that time it has become one of the most popular collectibles offered to the glass-conscious public. This glass has, with few exceptions, an outer surface that glows with a smooth satin matte finish, which was produced by subjecting the piece to hydrofluoric acid. Satin glass is composed of two layers, with the pattern showing through to the outside of the piece. Patterns are unlimited in number, but the ones most frequently found are the Diamond Quilted, Herringbone, Swirl and Raindrop. Satin glass was produced in one solid color, two colors blended, a single color shading light to dark, or a number of colors, making for added attractiveness.

The first reproductions of Satin glass to cause consternation among collectors appeared during the 1930's; others appeared about six years ago. These later pieces are easily recognized. Actually, they are so obviously new that they should not deceive anyone, because most of the shapes found in the new Satin glass are unlike any known old ones. It should also be noted that many pieces of the new ware have no specific pattern, but a considerable quantity of Diamond Quilted pieces are on the market, along with the Raindrop pattern and a very poor example of the Herringbone pattern.

The importers of this new Satin glass sell it as new Satin glass. Articles made in Italy are easy to identify, as the pieces are heavier and the layers of glass appear thick. Old pieces of Satin glass are exquisite in texture and light in weight. Satin glass produced in England is of better quality than the Italian. The glass is thinner and is lighter weight, and amateur collectors have been fooled by it. However, the distinct white (chalky) lining, rough texture, and the quality of the glass gives these new pieces away. Other distinguishing features of the new Satin glass are: 1) Thin reeded handles on the pitchers, which are too small in diameter when compared with the old (1 might add that these have been applied too clumsily). 2) The crimped top edges on the pitchers and vases are poorly done. Many show tell-tale tool marks, which never appear on the original old pieces. 3) Every piece of this new ware that I have examined has a rough pontil, often sharp enough to cut the finger. However, pieces that have been artificially aged are turning up with unpolished ground pontils.

Listed below are the new Satin glass pieces known to have been produced up to the present time. They can be found in the following colors: blue, yellow, pink, apricot, raspberry, green and red, with many examples shading to a light tan or white.

Bowls in various sizes (some footed), plain and decorated

Creamer and Sugar

Cruet

Fairy Lamp

Miniature Lamp

Pickle Castor

Pitchers, water and milk

Salt and Pepper Shakers

Toothpick Holder

Tumbler

Vases in various sizes

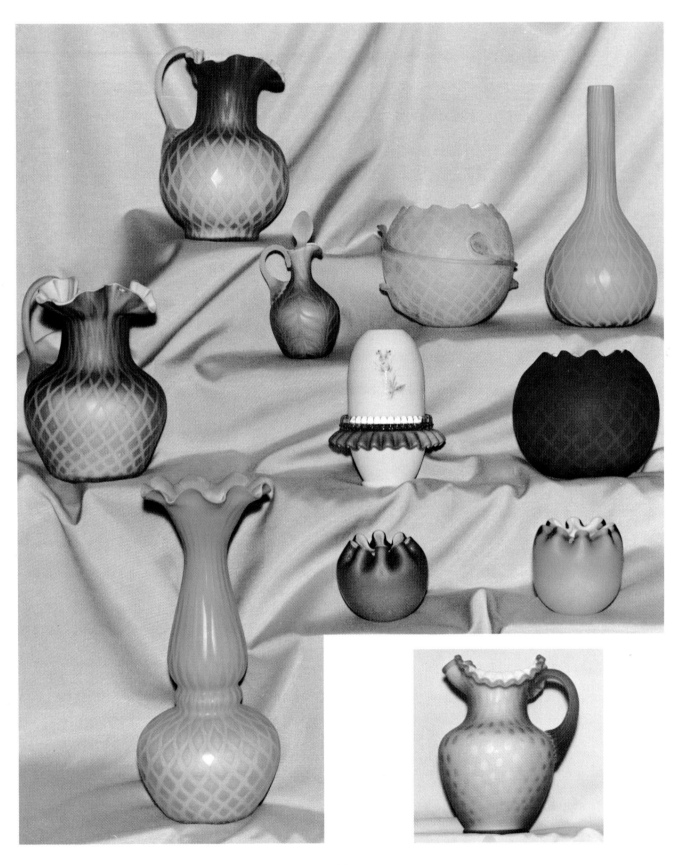

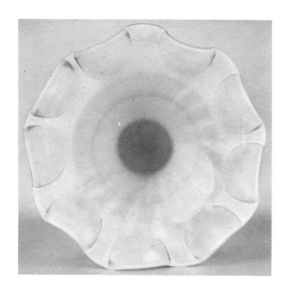

TOP VIEW OF REPRODUCED
M.O.P. VASE ILLUSTRATED ON
OPPOSITE PAGE. Note "U"
shaped crimped edge, not found
on 19th century pieces.

Reproduced Rose Bowl in the M.O.P. Herringbone
Pattern. (Note the poorly crimped edges.)

New Yellow Quilted Satin Glass with applied
decoration.

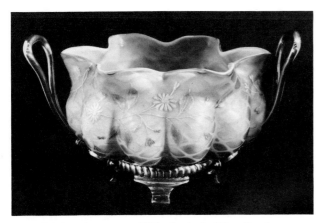

Origin unknown; ca. 1885. Bowl of pink satin glass, gilt decoration. Stand marked "Meridan B Company —1648". Courtesy of Corning Glass Center.

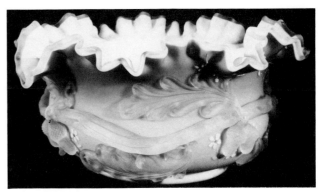

Origin unknown; ca. 1885. Bowl of satin glass with applied and enameled decoration; apricot lined with white. Courtesy of Corning Glass Center.

Origin unknown; ca. 1885. Blue satin glass bowl with "Herringbone" pattern. Stand marked "Derby Silver Co., Derby, Conn." Courtesy of Corning Glass Center.

Reproduced Cut Velvet Cruet, available in pink or blue. 7" tall. As far as it is known, only cruets have been reproduced in this pattern. They actually do not resemble the old ware close enough to make them appear genuine.

Satin Glass Rose Bowl. Courtesy of The Henry Ford Museum, Dearborn, Michigan.

SHADED OPALESCENT GLASSWARE

Shaded opalescent glassware is any glass which has raised opalescent white designs on its surface. It dates from the late nineteenth century, and was considered to be an inexpensive glass. It can be found in a multitude of patterns, with different background colors—ranging from transparent crystal on through the complete spectrum. The most popular patterns are Hobnail (type with opal hobs), Bullseye, Swirl and Spanish Lace.

STARS AND STRIPES

The popular "Stars and Stripes" pattern was originally produced by the Beaumont Glass Company of Martins Ferry, Ohio. The company was established in 1895 by Harry Northwood's brother-in-law, Percy J. Beaumont.

Reproduced barber bottles were made in this pattern several years ago, and new tumbers are currently being produced. Anyone who has seen examples from both centuries, should be able to recognize the the reproduction. The glass is of poorer quality (slick texture), the thickness varies, and the opalescent stars and stripes have a delicate bluish cast. And like the amberina tumblers, there is a "+" mold mark in the base. This is especially obvious when held to the light.

SPANISH LACE

Spanish Lace, with its clear, distinct opalescent flower and leaf pattern, belongs to the shaded opalescent glassware family. Many reproductions have been made in this pattern, in an array of colors with Vaseline and Cranberry pieces predominating. The new pieces are thick, and the design is diffused through the glass—giving the opalescent flowers and leaves a flowing appearance. This characteristic is not found in early pieces.

The known reproductions are:

    Barber Bottle
    Cruet
    Finger Bowl
    Pickle Jar
    Pitcher (Water and Milk)
    Sugar Shaker
    Syrup Pitcher

Opalescent Cranberry Coin Dot Pitcher and Tumbler. Made by Fenton Art Glass Co. Produced in 1947, and discontinued December 31, 1956.

Vase; American; ca. 1890-1900. Yellow with white pattern-molded flower-like design H. app. 10½". Usually called by collectors "Spanish Lace". Courtesy of Corning Glass Center.

Reproduced Stars and Stripes Tumbler

NEW SHADED OPALESCENT GLASSWARE

Wine Bottle

6" Vase

5" Vase

6" Vase

5" Vase

11½" Vase

8½" Fluted, Cranberry Opal Rib Barber Bottle

Cranberry Opal Swirl 4½" Sugar Shaker

8½" Fluted, Cranberry Opal Swirl Barber Bottle

Cranberry Spanish Lace Water Pitcher; Also made in Vaseline Color

6½" Cranberry Opal Honeycomb Milk Pitcher

Stars and Stripes Tumbler

Cranberry Opal Swirl Tumbler

Eye Dot Tumbler

Cranberry with Opal Overlay Tumbler in Honeycomb Pattern

Spanish Lace Tumbler. Colors: Cranberry or Vaseline

Opalescent Dot Tumbler

Cranberry Opal Swirl Water Pitcher; Also made in a 6½" size

Cranberry Opal Dot Water Pitcher; Also made in a 5½" tall Creamer

Cranberry Opal Honeycomb Water Pitcher

50

SPATTERGLASS, SPANGLED GLASS and VASA MURRHINA

Spattered, Spangled and Vasa Murrhina are three different types of glass, but much confusion exists in the proper definition of terms in this field of Art Glass.

"Spatterglass" consists of a variety of small pieces of different colored glass, which have been applied to a body of opaque white or transparent colored glass. This type of glass is also known as "Splashware" and "End of Day." However, experts avoid using the latter term as it has been established beyond all doubt that these variegated glasswares were actually production items, not objects that were produced at the end of the day from leftover pieces of glass which remained in the glassblowers pots.

"Spangled" glassware is frequently called "Vasa Murrhina," but knowledgeable collectors do not use this term because it does not apply to "Spangled" glassware. William Leighton, Jr., of Hobbs, Brockunier & Company, was issued a patent on January 29, 1884, covering his method or producing "Spangled" ware. Examples of this type of glass consist of metallic flakes embedded in opaque white or transparent colored glass.

"Vasa Murrhina" glassware was produced in quantity at the Vasa Murrhina Art Glass Company in Sandwich, Massachusetts, during the late nineteenth century. It is one of the most colorful glasswares produced during the nineteenth century. John C. DeVoy, Assignor to the Vasa Murrhina Art Glass Company, registered a patent on July 1, 1884, for a process of decorating glassware with particles of mica. The ware was named for the fabled "Vasa Murrhina" and it consists of embedded pieces of colored glass and mica flakes (coated with copper, gold, nickel or silver), sandwiched between an inner layer of glass which is opaque, and an outer layer of clear or transparent colored glass. It was also produced by other American glass firms and in England.

These types of Victorian Art Glass have all been reproduced in America as well as in European countries during recent years. The new examples are easily identified as they are thicker and heavier than earlier pieces, have pontil scars, colors are more garish, and shapes are modern.

Group of small pitchers produced by the Pilgrim Glass Corp., and listed in the 1969 catalog as "End of Day" glass.
All examples consist of milk-white pieces of glass on a transparent colored background of blue, red, amber or green glass.

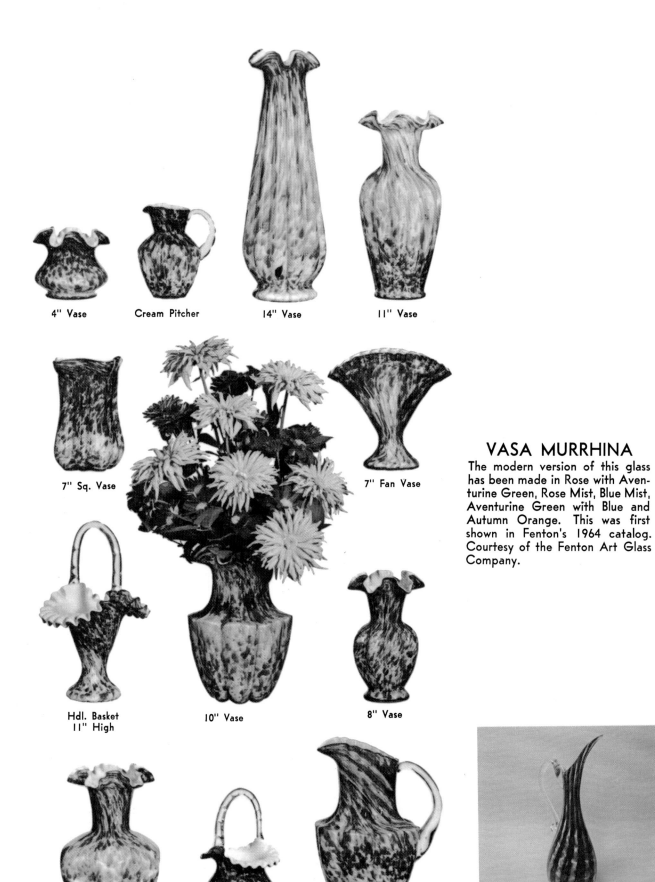

4" Vase

Cream Pitcher

14" Vase

11" Vase

7" Sq. Vase

7" Fan Vase

VASA MURRHINA
The modern version of this glass has been made in Rose with Aventurine Green, Rose Mist, Blue Mist, Aventurine Green with Blue and Autumn Orange. This was first shown in Fenton's 1964 catalog. Courtesy of the Fenton Art Glass Company.

Hdl. Basket
11" High

10" Vase

8" Vase

9" Pinch Vase DC

Hdl. Basket
7" High

Pitcher

New Vasa Murrhina Ewer

52

NEW STRETCH GLASS

Iridescent glass with a coarse "stretched" or "crackle" finish is being manufactured in West Germany, and shipped to several East coast jobbers. These items carry paper labels "West Germany," and when they are removed you have whatever the dealer wants to call it! Unfortunately, many pieces of this glass bear some resemblance to old designs (especially the plates), and the thousands of fine lines on its surface gives it a "puckered" effect, which reflects and refracts light, giving the glass its luminous quality. For this reason it has been attributed, erroneously, to American manufacturers. The glass has been regarded by some as Carnival glass, and by others as Tiffany, Aurene and Imperial "stretch" glass.

Happily, there are six distinguishing characteristics that identify this glass and they are: 1) lacks the brilliant luminous quality of the old glass; 2) coarse, rough, wavy texture; 3) plates have a thick foot rim on the bottom; 4) vases also have a thick bottom making them heavy; 5) vases are not completely iridized on the inside; frequently only a small portion of the bottom is covered, with sides appearing dull and unfinished; and 6) every piece of this ware that I have examined has a perfectly smooth, dull, ground pontil which varies in size from an inch to two inches in diameter.

The new stretched pieces can be found in ruby, blue, green and amber. The known pieces are:

Bowl, 6″ diam.

Hat Vases, 8½″, 6¾″, 6″, and 4¾″ diam.

Plates, 11″, 7½″ and 6¾″ diam.

Tumbler, 3½″ high

Vases with scalloped edges, 10″, 7″, and 6″ high

Vases with round tops, 10″, 7″, 6¼″ and 4½″ high

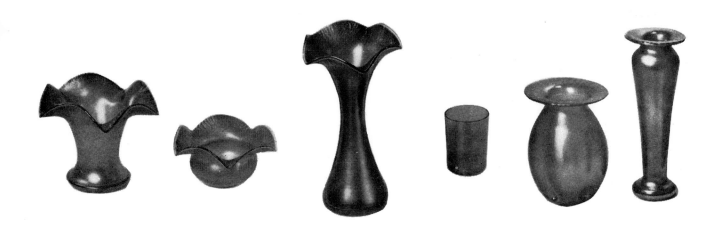

NEW RUBY "STRETCH" GLASS VASES AND TUMBLER

Numerous pieces of this new glass is showing up in antique shops, signed "L.C.T."
A very distinguishing characteristic of the ruby pieces is a greenish-yellow rim edge.
Note the light edge that appears on the vases illustrated.

REPRODUCTIONS:

Row 1: New "Stretch" glass Hat Vase

Row 2: "Stretch" Vase; Carnival Toothpick

Row 3: "Stretch" Vase and Plate; Coralene Vase

Row 4. Carnival Toothpicks; "Stretch" Plate

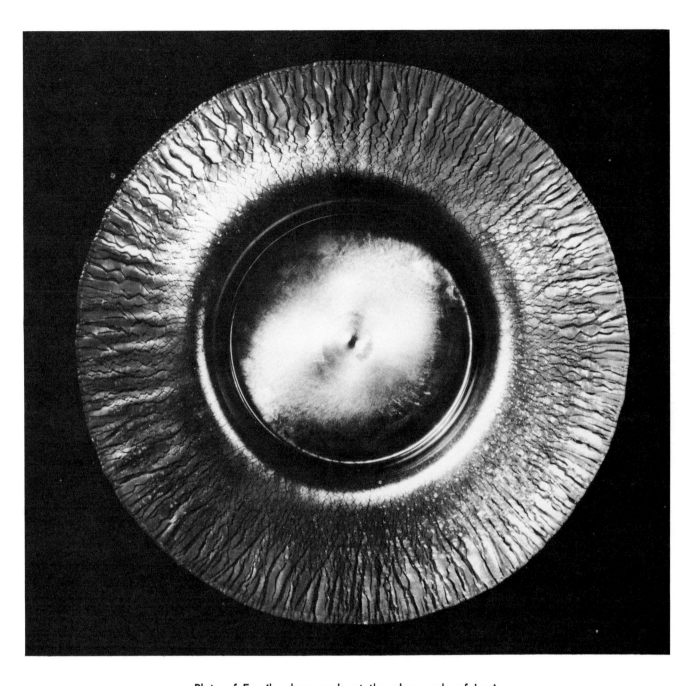

Plate of Favrile glass, made at the glass works of Louis
Comfort Tiffany. Early twentieth century, dia. 9½".
Courtesy of Corning Glass Center.

NEW STRETCH GLASS PLATE

VASELINE GLASS

The term "Vaseline" refers to color, as it resembles the greenish-yellow color typical of the oily petroleum jelly known as Vaseline. This ware was produced by French factories, as well as American art and pressed glass factories, during the 1870's. It was made in both clear and opaque yellow, and occasionally the two colors were combined in one piece; or Vaseline was combined with clear glass.

Numerous pressed glass reproductions have been made in Vaseline glass—especially the hobnail pattern.

NEW VASELINE GLASS WITH OPALESCENT HOBS
Courtesy of Imperial Glass Corp., Bellaire, Ohio

| Ice Tea Tumbler | Water Tumbler | Juice Tumbler | Pitcher/Vase | Cruet and Stopper | Handled Cruet and Stopper |

| Salt and Pepper Set | Goblet | Sherbert | Wine | Footed Sugar and Cream Set |

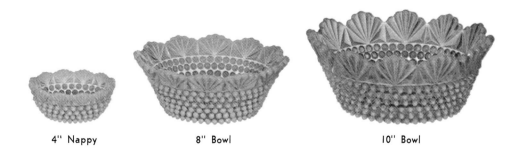

| 4" Nappy | 8" Bowl | 10" Bowl |

REPRODUCTIONS

Row 1: Rubina Toothpick; Opaline
         Glass Cruet
Row 2: LeGras Vase (French Cam-
         eo); Cut Overlay Vase
Row 3: Plated Amberina Water
         Pitcher
         Amberina Tumbler
         Nailsea Cruet
         Bohemian Vase

Row 4: Cranberry Swirl Creamer
         Coralene Vase
         Amberina Vase
Row 5: Cranberry Basket
         Rubina Verde Hobnail Cruet
         Aventurine Vase

SILVER PETTICOAT

a solid Turquoise color, inside and out, with a crystal edging. Courtesy of the Fenton Art Glass Company.

7" Bowl   5½" Bowl   Ftd. Comport   Handled Relish

13" Bowl

PEACHCREST

A deep pink glass interior cased with a Milk Glass exterior, then edged with crystal. This glass may be found with a blue color rather than pink and is referred to as Silver Jamestown. Courtesy of The Fenton Art Glass Company.

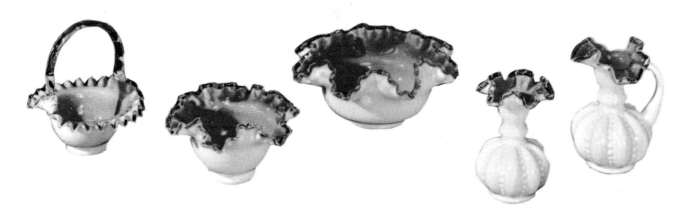

Three new vases introduced by the Fenton Company in 1968 are already considered by many to be collectible. Vases are available in Ebony, Orange, Orange Satin, Milk Glass, and French Opalescent. Courtesy of the Fenton Art Glass Co.

Mandarin Vase   Vessel of Gems Vase   Empress Vase

8" Overlay vases. Colors: Blue, Wild Rose, Apple Green, Honey Amber and Coral.

8" Bubble Optic Pinch vase. Colors: Blue, Rose, Green, Amber and Coral.

Candy Box. Colors: Blue, Rose, Green, Amber and Coral.

11½" Bubble Optic vase. Colors: Blue, Rose, Green, Amber and Coral.

7½" Bubble Optic vase. Colors: Blue, Rose, Green, Amber and Coral.

5" Vase

5" Wild Rose and Bowknot vase. Colors: Amber, Coral and Milk Glass.

"NEW" SHADED CABINET VASES (Burgundy shaded to lavender or Burgundy shaded to white). Made in Italy.

7½" Wild Rose and Bowknot vase. Colors: Blue, Rose, Milk Glass and Green.

Jacqueline Pattern. Made in a 6" vase, Sugar & Creamer, Salt & Pepper, Pansy Vase and a 48 oz. Pitcher. Colors: Blue, Green, Milk Glass and Rose.

Fenton Art Glass Pieces and Italian Vases.

60

Chapter II
PRESSED GLASS

PRESSED GLASS

Pressed glass is American in origin, and the method of pressing it into molds has been known since the time of the ancient Egyptians. However, it wasn't until the 1820's that ingenious Yankees invented and perfected machinery for successfully pressing glass. By 1845 pressed glass was a common household commodity, and it has been estimated that from about 1827 to around 1915, between 1500 and 2500 different patterns were produced. About 1865, manufacturers began to color their products using light and dark amber, apple green, turquoise, blue, vaseline, amethyst, ruby, black, carmel, custard, milk-white, opalescent in various tints, etc. Gold and silver gilt and colored stains were also used.

During the 70's and early 80's, the pressed glass industry reached the peak of its production, when there were literally hundreds of factories doing a profitable business. The era of this fascinating All American glass ended between 1895 and 1915, when everyone who could afford it began to buy cut glass.

Because of the widespread interest in pressed glass, collectors have just about exhausted the supply of original old pieces; so, many substitutes have been created, along with reproductions.

It would be impractical to attempt to write about the background of each of the patterns that has been copied through the years, as they have been discussed in detail in other books. However, I will cover those reproduced patterns which are causing the greatest confusion in the antique field today. In addition, I will give the reader as complete a listing as possible of all known reproduced patterns, listing each new piece that has been or is being produced, for easy reference. (Page 74). Although I have made an extensive effort to list all of the pieces, it is reasonably certain that I have missed some, because there have been copies produced that have not been sold extensively.

COIN

"New" United States Frosted Coin glass toothpicks produced in Japan with the 1892 date have been confusing collectors for about three years. Their frosting seems correct, not too white and opaque. These toothpick holders were also produced with a silvered coin, and they would never fool anyone but the amateur, as the coin has been sprayed or painted with chrome paint. Both toothpicks are heavier than the originals, and the

glass has an obvious glossy appearance of new glass. The stars on the new toothpick holders are larger than those on the original pieces, the letters on the coin are blurred to give a worn appearance, and the woman's features are too prominent. Another way to detect these new pieces is the shape of the eagle. It actually resembles a young pullet with upraised wings (low relief), instead of a full grown eagle.

Footed Frosted Coin spooners came on the market last year in clear glass, as well as in vaseline. Spooners were never produced in this shape originally, and were never made in vaseline glass. Surprisingly enough, the coins on the modern spooners are oval in shape.

DAISY AND BUTTON

There have been more reproductions made in the Daisy and Button pattern than any other single design. Since the pattern has been produced by several different factories with variations in detail, distinguishing between the old and the new is often difficult. Fortunately, all of the new glass has one common failing when held to the light, as the clear portions of the design have a "wavy" or "crinkly" appearance, regardless of form. It should be perfectly clear. In addition, the new Daisy and Button pieces are heavier, the colors deeper, buttons are sharper, rather than softly molded.

LION

The frosted Lion pattern has always been a popular pattern among collectors. It was produced by Gillinder & Sons of Philadelphia, Pennsylvania, in the 1870's. Like other frosted patterns reproduced during the 1930's, the satin finish on these pieces was chalklike, and the detail poor. But collectors have never had too much difficulty in telling the new from the old in this pattern, as the Lion appears to be very unhappy since he has been reproduced. The corners of his mouth sag downward, whereas on the original pieces his mouth is in a straight line and he has a pleasant expression on his face.

It will be of interest to add that amber Frosted Lion compotes were produced during the early 1960's by the Imperial Glass Company. Each compote is marked with the entwined "I G" on the base and inside the lid are the raised words "Patented Aug. 6th, 1889."

MOON AND STAR

The Moon and Star pattern has been reproduced so widely since the 1930's that no attempt has been made to list all known pieces and colors. The pattern was offered only in clear or clear and frosted glass originally. Because dimensions of pieces differ, the easiest way to judge a piece in this pattern is to have access to an authenticated nineteenth-century example. The early reproductions in Moon and Star included goblet, footed sauce dish, eggcup, colored goblet, clear champagne, covered butter, salt dip, sugar bowl, spoon holder, footed tumbler, water pitcher, plates in various sizes, punch bowl and punch cup.

RUBY THUMBPRINT

Originally this glass was made by both Adams & Company and Doyle & Company, both of Pittsburgh, Pennsylvania. It was known as "Excelsior" and was listed in catalogues as the "X L C R" pattern. It was produced during the 1890's, in all the usual pieces.

The reproduced pieces in this pattern are very good; however, the colored top portion hasn't been produced skillfully enough to deceive an experienced collector. Original pieces have a dark ruby red top, whereas the new ware produced today by Colony is a bright red, and has a metallic sheen.

THREE FACE

The Three Face pattern is well known to collectors. It was produced by George Duncan & Sons of Pittsburgh, Pennsylvania, during the 1870's. Early reproductions in this pattern appeared in the 1930's, and today new copies are being produced and sold by the L. G. Wright Glass Company of New Martinsville, West Virginia. It has never been difficult for collectors to recognize the early copies in this pattern, as the frosted finish is too white, and the texture is coarse and rough to the touch. In addition, the faces lack the distinctive clarity of detail that is found on the original examples. The frosting on all of the new pieces being produced today appears very authentic. It is grayish-white, smoother, and feels soft when touched. However, the faces (often slightly crooked) are not right, especially in the shape of the nose. In addition, the hairline lacks detail, and the eyes frequently appear blurred or sunken.

WESTWARD-HO

Westward-Ho pattern glass was designed by a German mold maker named Jacobus, who was associated with Gillinder & Sons, of Philadelphia, and ranked as one of the best of his day. The Gillinder factory was established in 1861, and produced the Westward-Ho pattern shortly after the Centennial of 1876.

This ware was originally named "Pioneer" because the frosted or satin finish was applied in the Pioneer Room. The component parts of the Westward-Ho design can be traced to the pioneer west of the Currier & Ives prints.

Deceptive pieces have appeared on the market from time to time since the 1930's and, until recently, they have been easy to spot, as the frosted finish was much too white, dry and harsh to the touch. The quality of the frosting has improved so much that it is almost identical to the original, both in appearance and texture. However, the poor detail of the pattern itself hasn't changed, which makes the new ware easy to recognize when carefully examined. The deer's body, as well as the buffalo's, is almost completely without hair on the copies; whereas on the original old pieces the hair is clearly defined. Another clue in identifying the new from the old is the deer's mouth which appears closed, always in a straight line, on the original glass.

This charming old pattern was made only in clear and frosted glass. However, in recent years some of the reproduced goblets have been found in amethyst, blue, and green glass.

New Westward-Ho pieces on the market today are:

Celery

Covered Butter

Creamer

Goblet

Sherbert

Sugar (covered)

Wine

The majority of reproductions can be easily detected, once you know what to look for. The following tips will be helpful in recognizing the old glass from the spurious:

1. The sense of touch is, at times, very revealing, especially in identifying new glass. If genuinely old, glass will not have sharp edges; edges will have been rounded by time. However, on oc-

casion a piece of glass turns up with frosted mold lines. This indicates that the sharp edges have been ground off to simulate wear.

2. The surface of old glass possesses a soft dullness, whereas new glass is brilliant looking.

3. Not every piece of old glass will ring, so don't depend upon this factor as a reliable test. Many pieces of old glass do have an excellent tone, however, due to the thickness, shape and base.

4. Many patterns have been produced in colors today that are not found in the old glass.

5. Examine with care pitcher handles as well as lips, rims and bases on objects. These areas will acquire a soft worn appearance from usage, and practically every piece of old glass will show some telltale maze of wear scratches.

6. Oftentimes there are discrepancies in shape as well as in design, which differ from the original pattern. Compare your pattern with those shown in books and you will be able to learn more about its characteristics.

7. Weight plays a very important part in identifying the new glass from the old. Most reproductions are heavier; however, there are some pieces that are lighter in weight, such as the new custard, hobnail and lacy sandwich pieces, for example.

8. A reproduction is usually less costly than an original because, as yet, most dealers haven't had the courage to ask the "antique" price. Be very cautious, as bargains can be expensive when buying antiques. This is the first, and sometimes costliest, lesson all collectors have to learn.

Original Westward-Ho Goblet

Reproduced Goblet, Made in 1968

Coin Glass Spooner made in clear and Vaseline. Spooners were never produced in this shape originally.

Reproduced Coin Glass Toothpick Holder Made in Japan.

REPRODUCED 15 PIECE DAISY AND BUTTON PUNCH SET

Courtesy of The L. E. Smith Glass Company

65

L to R—New Three Face Pattern glass toothpick holder, never made originally. On the right is an original Salt Dip in the Three Face Pattern.

"New" Childs ABC Plate. Made in Crystal, Blue, Green and Vaseline.

Butter dish and cover, Westward Ho. After 1876; Phila. glassworks of James Gillinder & Sons. Courtesy of Corning Glass Center.

Covered sugar bowl in Three Face Pattern. Courtesy of Corning Glass Center.

CONFUSING "NEW" PIECES

"NEW" AMBER "ATTERBURY" LION BOX AND COVER. Bears the Imperial Trademark on bottom, and mark on inside of cover reads "Pat. Aug. 6th, 1889."

Amberina Canoe in Daisy and Button Pattern.

Pickle Jars in Daisy and Button Pattern.

Amethyst Hen with Milk Glass Head.

7" Milk Glass Hen with Amethyst Head.

11" Milk Glass Atterbury Duck with Amethyst Head.

6½" Covered Duck Dish: Colors: Amberina, Blue Amber and Amethyst with Milk Glass Head.

10" Hen on Nest

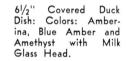

14" Gold and White Hen and Rooster.

5" Covered Turkey. Made in Amberina, Blue and Amber.

5" Rooster on Nest. Colors: Amberina, Blue, Amber and Purple Slag.

5" Hen on Nest. Colors: Amberina, Blue Amber and Slag.

5" Bird on Nest. Colors: Amberina, Blue and Amber.

MORE "NEW" PIECES

11" Purple Slag Atterbury Duck.

11" Amethyst Atterbury Duck with Milk Glass Head.

11" Amethyst Atterbury Duck.

11" Milk Glass Atterbury Duck.

"NEW" RUBY THUMBPRINT, BY COLONY

Sugar and Creamer Set

Sherbet   Wine   Goblet

Dessert

"NEW" 5" Wedding Bowl
with Cover

"NEW" 8" Salad Plate

"NEW" Cup and Saucer

Reproduced Lion
Pattern Goblet

Reproduced Three
Face Pattern
Sherbert

Reproduced Three
Face Pattern 6"
Covered Compote

Reproduced Three
Face Pattern
Goblet

Reproduced Westward
Ho Pattern 6"
Covered Compote
with High Finial

Reproduced Westward
Ho Pattern 6" Oval
Covered Compote

Reproduced 10½" Lion
Bread Plate

Reproduced Three
Face Pattern Wine

REPRODUCED PRESSED GLASS PATTERNS
and Color Chart

A—Amber
B—Blue
C—Clear
F—Frosted
G—Green
M—Milk-white
P—Pink
R—Ruby
S—Slag
T—Turquoise
V—Vaseline
Y—Yellow

AM—Amethyst
AR—Amberina
BM—Blue Milk Glass
CR—Cranberry
CU—Custard
DB—Dark Blue
RB—Rubina Verde

(Whenever an asterisk (*) precedes the name of a pattern, it designates that it was originally produced in clear glass).

ALPHABET PLATE
8″ Plate, girls head in center (B, C, G, V)

*ACTRESS
Pickle Jar (C)

*BABY FACE
Compote (C)
Goblet (C)
Sugar Bowl (C)
Wine (C)

*BALTIMORE PEAR
Butter Dish (C)
Cake Stand (C)
Celery (C)
Creamer (C)
Goblet (C)
Pitcher, water (C)
Sauce, small footed (C)
Sugar bowl (C)

BASKETWEAVE
Goblets (A, B, C, G, Y)
Pitcher, water (A, B, C, G, Y)

BEADED GRAPE
Compote, square covered (A, AM, B, G)
Goblet (C & G)
Plate, large square (C & G)
Sauce, square (A, AM, B, G)
Tumbler (G)
Wine (G)

BLACKBERRY
Butter Dish (C & M)
Celery (C & M)
Creamer (C & M)
Egg Cup, single (M)
Goblet (C & M)
Pitcher, creamer (C & M)
Sugar Bowl (C & M)

*BROKEN COLUMN
Goblet (C)

*CABBAGE LEAF (frosted)
Butter Dish (C)
Celery (C)
Creamer (C)
Goblet (C)
Sugar Bowl (C)
Wine (A & B)

*CABBAGE ROSE
Goblet (C)

*CHECKERBOARD
Honey Dish, square and footed (C & M)

*CHERRY
Butter, covered (A, AM, G)
Creamer (A, AM, B, G, R, V, BM, CU)
Goblet (A, B, C, G, R, V)
Salt Dip (A, AM, AR, B, G)
Sugar Bowl (A, AM, AR, B, G)
Toothpick Holder (A, AM, AR, B, BM, CU, G, P, R)
Tumbler (A & B)
Pitcher, water (A, B, R)

*COIN (U. S. Dollar)
Toothpick Holder (C & F, or with painted silver dollar)
Spooner, footed (not made originally)

*CRYSTAL WEDDING
Goblet (clear, and clear decorated in red)
Compote, covered (same as above)

*DAISY AND BUTTON WITH NARCISSUS
Bowls in various sizes, round and oval (C)
Vases in various sizes (A, C, DB, G, Y)

DIAMOND QUILTED
Goblet (A, B, G, AM, R)

EMERALD GREEN HERRINGBONE
Goblet (A, B, G, AM, R)

*EYE WINKER
 Butter, covered (A & G)
 Bowl, footed (A, G, R)
 Creamer (A, C, G, R)
 Pickle dish (A & G)
 Pitcher, water (A, B, G, R)
 Salt Dip (A, G, R)
 Sauce (A, B, G, R)
 Shakers, salt and pepper (A, B, C, G, R)
 Toothpick Holder (A, G, R)
 Tumbler (A, B, G, R)
 Vase, 6″ (A, B, G, R)

*FROSTED ARTICHOKE
 Goblet (C)

*FROSTED CIRCLE
 Goblet (C)

*GOOSEBERRY
 Goblet (C)

*GRASSHOPPER
 Goblet (C)

HOBNAIL
 1. Fan Top Hobnail
  a. Bowl (A, B, P)
  b. Sauce (A, B, P)

 *2. Flattened Hobnail
  a. Tumbler (C)

 3. Opalescent Hobnail
  a. Baskets, in various sizes (CR, DB, V)
  b. Bowls, in various sizes (CR, DB, V)
  c. Cruet (CR, DB, RV, V)
  d. Goblet (CR, B, V)
  e. Pitchers, in various sizes
  f. Sauce (CR, B, V)
  g. Shakers, salt and pepper (CR, B, V)
  h. Tumbler (CR, DB, P, V)
  i. Vases, in various sizes (CR, B, P, V)
  j. Wine (CR, B, V)

 4. Pointed Hobnail
  Barber Bottles (A, B, C, CR, G, AM, AR, RB, V)
  Bowls, in various sizes (A, B, C, CR, G)
  Cup and Saucer (A, B, C, G, V)
  Mug (A, B, C, G, V)
  Pickle Castor (A, B, C, CR, G, V)
  Pitchers, in various sizes (A, B, C, CR, G, V)
  Sauce (A, B, C, CR, G, V)
  Shakers, salt and pepper (A, B, C, CR, G, V)

Sugar Bowl (A, B, C, CR, G, V)
Tumbler (A, B, C, CR, G, V)
Vinegar Cruet (A, B, CR, G, V)
Wine (A, B, C, CR, V)

*HORN OF PLENTY
 Goblet (C)
 Tumbler (C)

*HORSESHOE
 Platter, 10x14″ (C)

*IVY IN SNOW
 Butter Dish (C)
 Cake Stand (C)
 Celery (C)
 Creamer (C)
 Goblet (C)
 Pitcher (C)
 Sugar Bowl (C)

JERSEY SWIRL
 Goblet (A, B, C, G, R)
 Compote, covered (A, B, G, AR)
 Plate (B & C)
 Salt Dip (A, B, G, AM, R)
 Sauce (A & B)

KING'S CROWN (known as Ruby Thumprint when colored)
 Compote (C)
 Cordial (C)
 Goblet (C)
 Wine (C)

*LATE PANELED GRAPE
 Goblet (C)

*LION
 Bread Plate 10½″
 Butter Dish
 Celery
 Compote, oval covered
 Cordial
 Egg Cup
 Goblet
 Pitcher, water
 Sauce
 Sugar Bowl

MAPLE LEAF
 Goblet (A, B, C, F, G, AM)

*NEW ENGLAND PINEAPPLE
 Goblet (C)
 Wine (C)

*PANELED DAISY
Goblet (C)
Tumbler (C)

*PANELED GRAPE
Bowl, crimped 12" (R)
Butter Dish (C)
Celery (C)
Cordial (C)
Compote, covered (A, B, G)
Creamer (A, B, C, G, AM, R)
Goblet (A, G, M, R)
Pitcher, water (C & R)
Plates, in various sizes (C & R)
Sauce (C)
Sugar (A, B, C, G, AM, R)
Spooner (C)
Wines (C)

*PLEAT AND PANEL
Goblet (C)
Plate, 7½ square (C)

*PLUME
Goblet (C)

*PRISCILLA
Compotes, in various sizes (A, B, C, G, R), covered
Goblet (A, B, C, G, R)
Rose Bowl (A, B, C, G, R)
Sauce (A, C, G)
Toothpick Holder (A, AM, B, G, R)
Wine (A, B, C, G, R)

RED BLOCK
Goblet (C)
Wine (C)

*RIBBON
Goblet (C)

*ROMAN ROSETTE
Goblet (C)

ROSE SPRIG
Goblet (A, B, C, Y)

ROSE IN SNOW
Goblet (A, B, C, V)
Mug (A, B, C, V)
Plate, 9" (A, B, C, V)

RUBY THUMBPRINT
Cake Plate, on standard
Compote, covered on standard
Cordial
Cup and Saucer

Goblet
Lemonade (never made originally)
Sherbet (never made originally)
Tumbler, small (never made originally)

*SAWTOOTH
Goblet (P)
Ice Tea, (P) never made originally
Sherbet (P)
Wine (P)

*STIPPLE STAR
Goblet (A, AM, C, G, R)
Pitcher, creamer (A, AM, C, G, R)
Salt Dip (A, AM, AR, C, G)
Sugar, covered (A, AM, B, C, R)
Wine, footed (A, AM, B, C, G, R)

THOUSAND EYE
Cruet, plain stem (A, B, C, G, V)
Goblet (A, B, C, G, V)
Mug (A, B, C, G, V)
Plate, 8" square (A, B, C, G, V)
Toothpick Holder (A, B, C, G, V)
Wine (A, B, C, G, V)

*THREE FACE
Butter Dish, covered
Cake Stand
Champagne
Claret
Compote, covered 6½", small
Creamer
Goblet
Lamp
Salt Dip
Sauce
Shakers, salt and pepper
Sugar Bowl
Toothpick Holder (records do not indicate that this was made originally)
Wine

*TULIP WITH SAWTOOTH
Wine (C)

TWO PANEL
Goblet (A, B, C, G, Y)
Wine (A, B, C, G, Y)

WILDFLOWER
Goblet (A, B, C, G, Y)
Plate, 10" (A, B, C, G, Y)
Sauce, footed, round (A, B, C, G, Y)
Tumbler (A, B, C, G, Y)
Wine (A, B, C, G, Y)

Chapter III
POTTERY and PORCELAIN

POTTERY and PORCELAIN

The opportunities for collecting pottery and porcelain are almost unlimited; however, these fields, like all others, are fraught with perils.

It is only through study, observation and inspection that serious collectors learn to determine a spurious piece from an authentic piece.

There is no direct method for the beginning collector to follow in achieving expert proficiency within a short time; however, there are eight basic rules which are helpful:

1. Concentrate on one field and do extensive research on your chosen subject.

2. Most public libraries have excellent illustrated books on pottery and porcelain, including their marks. Museums can often supply illustrated booklets on these subjects; however, there is usually a small charge for this service.

3. Study photographs of the pieces you want to collect. In addition, study marks until you can recognize easily the characteristics. A working knowledge of them is necessary in order to identify genuine pieces, as well as reproductions.

4. Buy several authentic pieces from reliable sources and use these as a basis for comparison with the pieces you plan to purchase. An authentic piece of pottery or porcelain will expose the reproduction, as there is always a marked contrast, whether it be in style, decoration or quality.

5. Collectors must learn the differences between traces of wear (scratches from natural daily use) and marks which have been applied artificially to simulate wear. Scratches or a dull area on the underside of an unmarked piece of pottery or porcelain indicates that a mark has been removed.

6. Dealers are usually willing to advise, and many take pride in actually assisting collectors; therefore, don't be afraid to ask questions. However, it is always wise to remember (and this applies to all fields of collecting) that few dealers know enough about more than one field of antiques to distinguish a reproduction from an authentic piece. Therefore, search for a dealer who is an authority on pottery and porcelain; for instance, don't consult the nearest dealer who has specialized in antique furniture and who has only a superficial knowledge about pottery or porcelain.

7. Don't buy a piece of pottery or porcelain (this also applies to objects made of glass) under poorly lighted conditions, unless you are prepared to be deceived, because many early pieces have been damaged through natural wear or accidental breakage. The true color, as well as any defects, are visible only under ideal lighting conditions (bright daylight). And be very cautious about buying a dirty object. Grime is an ideal camouflage.

8. It is never wise to buy pieces which are damaged or poorly mended because they may be reasonably priced. Although practically any piece of pottery or porcelain can be restored to its original beauty, the cost of repairing will increase the final price to that of a perfect piece.

BEAUMONT HERITAGE POTTERY

Beaumont Heritage Pottery was established in 1970 by Jerry Beaumont. Upon completing school at New York College of Ceramics at Alfred University, Beaumont began producing salt-glazed pottery and in 1975 moved to Portsmouth, New Hampshire. Here, he set up the pottery works in Strawberry Banke Historic Preservation — producing a variety of outstanding salt-glazed wares, many of which are illustrated. All decorations are done in cobalt blue.

MARKINGS FOR THE COLLECTOR

1970 - 1973 Stamp	"J. Beaumont" Huntington, L.I.	Initial on Bottom
1973 - 1975	"J. Beaumont" Alfred, N.Y.	J.B.
		Cross (†) & JB
1975 - Present	"Beaumont Pottery" Portsmouth, N.H.	
	J. Beaumont Portsmouth, N.H.	Cross (†) & JB
(approx. 1,000 pieces)	J. Beaumont Strawberry Banke, N.H.	

DECORATORS
C.R. — Chris Robinson
D.W. — Dorma West
C.C. — Christian Colby
E.P. — Erica Pyle
B.W. — Bobbie Warthold
P.W. — Pat Wallace

Markings to aid the collector in identifying Beaumont Pottery.

Courtesy Beaumont Heritage Pottery

BELLEEK

Some say it was the leprechauns who led the way. Others, less romantic, insist it was a certain John Caldwell Bloomfield who made the historic discovery.

Whichever it was, it all happened over a hundred years ago in a remote and beautiful part of Ireland. In the heart of County Fermanagh, on the banks of the River Erne, near the pastoral village of Belleek, a native clay deposit was found which proved to have qualities unlike any other clay in the world!

At first, the artisans who worked with clay to produce fine china were merely pleased with the pure, new source of raw material. But, the more they experimented with Belleek clay, the more astounded they became at its remarkable—almost magical—properties.

With this incredible clay, they could do things previously thought impossible. They could create china with a soft, almost creamy mother-of-pearl effect with spun-sugar designs that seemed almost too delicate to touch. But, to their amazement, the pieces retained a tough resilience that could withstand continuous daily use.

The craftsmen were jubilant and began to develop the unique designs and patterns for Belleek ware.

The Belleek Works was established in 1857, and today, just as a century ago, Irish Belleek china is made in buildings within walking distance of the original clay pits, according to the skills and traditions of the original artisans of so many years ago. And to those of Irish heritage, its appeal is irresistible and enchanting.

Belleek is world famous for its thinness and delicacy. Though it is almost gossamer in appearance, it is not unduly fragile. Its most distinctive feature is its nacreous or mother-of-pearl glaze, and some of the ware is embellished in soft pastel colors.

Generally speaking, Belleek production is confined either to relief molding or elaborate open work effects. The inspiration for many of its designs is based on objects associated with the nearby Irish Sea in the form of sea shells, corals, sea horses and marine plants. Mythology and Irish folklore also influenced its creations; thus the Neptune Tritons and leprechauns, and the modeling of some of its most popular patterns is inspired by the Limpet and Tridacna, both of the oyster family.

In some of the ornamental ware colored decorations are based on the beautiful Celtic designs in the Book of Kells.

The body of Belleek China consists of a prefused flux composed of feldspar, flint and alkalies, mixed with china and ball clays. The glaze contains white and red lead, flint and borax.

Slip casting is the method used for forming the ware. The slip is prepared by grinding the ingredients against granite blocks for six days. The slip is poured in warmed plaster molds and immediately poured out. What remains adhering to the mold sides is sufficient to form the delicate tableware which is of egg-shell thinness. Twenty minutes are allowed for setting the clay to "cheese" hardness, after which the molds are removed. The biscuit is then fired for 56 hours. The glazed ware is again fired and, where colors are applied, there are as many as four firings.

One of the most famous of Belleek creations is their open trellis work, which began around 1887. For this, clay at "cheese" hard stage is extruded in small rods, similar to spaghetti, which the craftsman lays over a plaster shape, interlacing them, keeping the whole process pliable by laying a damp cloth over the work until completed. The intricate flowers and other motifs are then applied —every flower being built up from the core— every petal added individually. The trellis or strap work in early baskets is slightly thicker and appears in rows of three. These pieces are marked with an applied Parian ribbon, impressed with the name Belleek Co., Fermanagh. Other older forms are also thicker and many are darker and have a grayish-yellow tinge, a sign of respectable age. The lustre is often worn or washed off in spots and is more subdued with a mother-of-pearl glow.

It would be a lasting delight to all collectors— and dealers—if all manufacturers were as consistent with their markings as this company has been. Between 1861 and 1890 the mark most frequently used was a transfer printed in black, brown, red or blue. The mark is an Irish wolfhound at the left, a round tower, and a harp at the right. Beneath it runs a ribbon bearing the name Belleek, with shamrocks. When the word Ireland is combined in the mark, this indicates manufacture after 1891. A circular Celtic Symbol was added in 1915, and was used with the mark until 1940, when the production of Belleek stopped (during World War II). The company resumed full production in 1946 and, since that time, when a piece of this ware is pronounced perfect, it is given the Belleek Hallmark: the Belleek name and site, and a representation of an Irish wolfhound, a harp, round tower and shamrock—in **GREEN.**

"NEW" BELLEEK PARIAN CHINA
All pieces illustrated were manu-
factured by Belleek Pottery Ltd.,
Belleek Co., Fermanagh, Ireland.
Courtesy of Waterford Glass Inc.,
New York.

BREININGER POTTERY

Lester and Barbara Breininger of Robesonia, Pa., are true folk artists of the twentieth century. During the last decade they have earned national recognition for their fine slip-decorated redware and sgraffito pottery. In addition to a variety of plates, they also make flowerpots, small cachepots, bowls, tumblers, mugs, wall plaques, crocks, vases, coffeepots and whimsical pieces, such as Christmas ornaments and Easter eggs. Barbara adds her skill and artistic ability in the decoration of their sgraffito ware.

After a piece of the Breininger pottery has been decorated, Lester signs and dates the item on the underside. Additionally, he frequently adds comments about the weather and, on occasion, mentions who is the current president of the United States.

Although all forms of redware are very collectible, the most desirable objects are the slip-decorated pieces, or the exceedingly rare "sgraffito" examples which have scratched or incised line decoration. This type decoration was for ornamentation, since examples were rarely used for ordinary utilitarian purposes, but were usually given as gifts. Decoration ranged from Pennsylvania Dutch inscriptions to elaborate motifs. Flowers and birds were the most typical decoration, in addition to animals and human figures showing wedding couples or a spirited horseman.

Examples of sgraffito pottery by Lester and Barbara Breininger.

DEDHAM POTTERY REPRODUCTIONS

The Dedham Pottery Company of Dedham, Massachusetts was famous for its crackleware dishes. Production began about 1895, and because of its popularity, over fifty patterns of tableware were made which picture blue outlines of animals, flowers and other motifs on a crackled gray ground. The two marks which identify this ware are: (1) the front-view outline of a rabbit; (2) the side view of a rabbit and the words DEDHAM POTTERY with a square, oftentimes impressed or painted.

Charlotte Starr, president of the Potting Shed Enterprise located at Concord, Mass., and her sons, Chris and Rob, are reproducing very impressive pieces of new Dedham Pottery in a variety of shapes and sizes. Like the originals, the new ware is entirely handcrafted, but only the rabbit pattern is being produced. The Starrs sign their pottery * (star) 77 on the backside to distinguish it from the original pottery.

78

GAME SETS

Game sets are decorated with pictures of birds or wild game, each depicted in its natural habitat. Most came in sets of twelve, plus a serving platter, and were made during the 1800's of fine porcelain, such as French Limoges, English Minton, or German porcelain. Signed sets of superlative quality are fetching astronomical prices and are sought after by collectors as they are an extremely decorative addition to any home.

The new game sets found today in gift shops and department stores (especially around the holidays), haven't given collectors any problem, but the game plates shown in this chapter have, because their quality is good, their mark is a confusing one, and they can be artificially aged very easily with fine steel wool, thus giving the gold trim a dull worn appearance that indicates years of usage.

This mark appears on many new plates today (game, bird, fruit and others), causing much confusion among collectors.

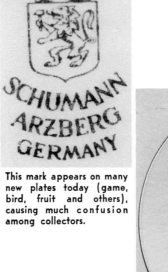

79

REPRODUCED KEWPIE DOLLS

Rose O'Neal's illustrations of Kewpies first appeared in The Ladies' Home Journal in 1909. Her charming little characters with hand painted features, topnots and fat round little tummies, became an immediate success. Kewpie dolls began to appear about 1913. They were made with legs together or with the legs apart, and some had jointed legs. Their eyes glance either to the right or to the left, and the surface of their bodies feels smooth when touched. The reproduced examples illustrated have a rough texture and they look new.

Reproduced Kewpies made in Japan

MUSTACHE CUPS

The mustache cup became popular after the war with Mexico, when men from lowest to highest rank cultivated the hair growth of the upper lip. These cups were made for drinking tea or coffee. Part of the rim of a mustache cup has a fixed cover with a small opening through which a man can drink without dipping his mustache into the liquid.

The first factory to make a mustache cup was Harvey Adams and Company of Longton, Staffordshire, England. During the years that followed, these cups were made by most of the famous factories from demitasse size to the quart size. Left-handed cups were also made, but they are a rarity. The mustache cup was usually made to order for the individual, and was made in silver, porcelain and pottery. The decade of the greatest vogue of these cups was the 1890's and, by the

turn of the century, both the cup and the mustache were out of style.

New right-handed, as well as left-handed, china mustache cups and saucers are being marketed today in sets. These examples are made in Japan and are marked on the base with a blue anchor, and above this (in blue) the word "BRANDEN-BURG."

SHAVING MUGS

H. P. & W. E. Taylor of Philadelphia distributed the earliest known shaving mug in the 1840's. These were accepted nationally, and were popular well into the 20th century, when the safety razor ended barbershop shaving business.

Barbershops favored shaving mugs, and many clients had personalized ones. Usually they were kept at a barbershop and the owner chose the decoration that illustrated his occupation and then had his name placed on the cup. There were more than 150 decorative patterns that indicated occupations and the more elusive ones, such as a mug showing a doctor, ball player or an undertaker, are quite rare and command a high price when found.

Actually, owning a personal shaving mug was something of a fad, but a man who owned one had succeeded in the eyes of his contemporaries and, to him, his shaving mug was a status symbol.

New occupational shaving mugs are being made today, but were not marketed in time to be included in this chapter.

New Scuttle Mug Marked

Shaving Mug marked "Brandenburg"
Made in Japan

Old Foley

JAMES KENT LTD
STAFFORDSHIRE
ENGLAND

This mark (in blue) appears on the underside of the reproduced
Mustache Cups, Shaving Mugs, and some of the Scuttle Mugs.

New "unmarked" China Barber Bottles

Old Mustache Cup
Courtesy of The Henry Ford Museum, Dearborn, Michigan

R. S. PRUSSIA

R. S. Prussia is the mark and the trade word for the Reinhold Schlegemilch firm of Surl, Germany, producers of quality china during the late 1880's. After 1891 the word Germany was substituted for Prussia. The majority of this ware (similar to that of Haviland and Limoges) was factory decorated; however, many German artists worked in their own homes and, occasionally, a piece is found bearing the name or initials of the artist.

Prices for R. S. Prussia have skyrocketed during the past five years, and rumors have been flying across the country for months that it is being reproduced. Those who have actually seen copies have told me that the quality of the china is very poor, but the mark is good. So—I diligently searched for a piece of the "new" ware and came up with nothing. Then, quite by accident, the mystery surrounding Prussia was solved.

While browsing in an antique shop (we almost didn't stop), I noted that the dealer displayed many lovely pieces of R. S. Prussia. I casually asked if she had seen any of the reproduced pieces, and she cheerfully proceeded to tell me that R. S. Prussia had never been copied—but the mark has been reproduced. She showed me a sheet of 140 R. S. Prussia decals, which sell for $14.00, complete with firing instructions. I was shocked! Here, before me, was a mark so skillfully produced, it would fool any collector or dealer—and suddenly the Prussia puzzle began to take shape, because it would be very easy to apply one of these decals to a piece of unmarked china, regardless of the quality, and pawn it off as an original piece of R. S. Prussia.

From this dear little lady I was able to obtain the name and address of a West coast distributor, and within two weeks I received a sheet of the decals. By comparing the old mark with the new, you will note that each letter (red) in the new mark has more modern characteristics, which gives it away.

THIS 11½" PLATE HAS CONFUSED COLLECTORS AS IT RESEMBLES AN R.S.PRUSSIA PLATE in the "Melon Boy" group. It is marked "Germany" and may also carry a mark that reads "Made in West Germany."

An original R.S.Prussia Bowl

An original R.S.Prussia Mark

Enlargement of reproduced R.S.Prussia
Mark.

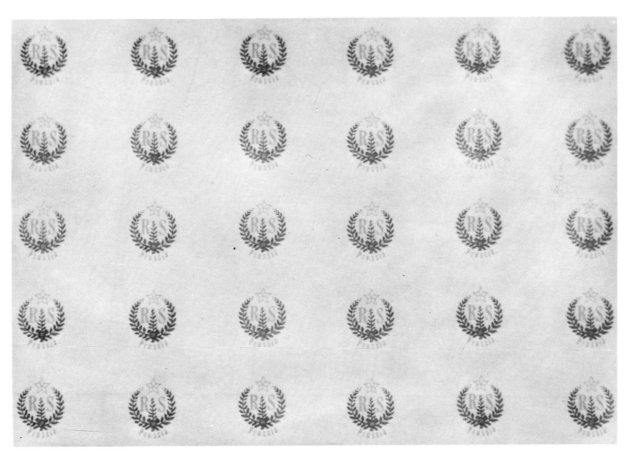

Reproduced R.S.Prussia Marks. These decals are sold in sheets containing 140
marks. Note the modern characteristics
in the lettering.

Chocolate Set with various pieces bearing reproduced R.S.Prussia mark. This set was made in Japan and the pattern is "Gold Medallion." All pieces were marked (in gold lettering) "Royal Crown." Once the mark was removed it became R.S.Prussia.

SPATTERWARE

Weaver's Ceramic Mold Company of New Holland, Pa. specializes in the reproduction of authentic Early American quality molds. Items illustrated here are but a small representation of the many different molds made by them. When decorated comparably to an early or original piece, objects look very authentic. However, it is easy to distinguish the new item, because it looks new, and, when placed side-by-side with an original piece, the new form is slightly smaller. It is with the passage of time and with usage that these new wares will confuse the novice. Weaver's molds are unmarked.

Mary Weaver has decorated many pieces, including a variety of beautiful spatterware items, some of which are included here. These pieces resemble tableware produced in Staffordshire, Scotland, and Wales during the last century for the American market. Very few pieces were marked. Although much of this now highly collectible ware was sent to New England and various points farther south, to this day, spatterware like Gaudy Dutch and Gaudy Welsh, is regarded everywhere as being characteristically "Pennsylvania Dutch," because of its popularity among the German settlers.

The term "spatter" describes the effect achieved, rather than the actual technique used, in decorating this type tableware. The "spattering" was done with either a sponge or a brush containing a moderate supply of the liquid color, which was tapped repeatedly against the piece to be decorated.

Items decorated by Mary Weaver are very collectible, because of their fine quality decoration. All objects decorated by Mrs. Weaver are marked (impressed) M.E.W.

84

New pieces of spatterware decorated by Mary E. Weaver.

NEW SPONGEWARE POTTERY

Spongeware, as it is known, is a decorative white earthenware made by applying the color — usually blue, blue/green, blue/brown, brown/tan/blue — to a white clay base. The object is then bathed in clear alkaline glaze. Because the desired hue was often-times applied with a color-soaked sponge, the term "spongeware" became common for this ware. Bowls, pitchers, bean pots and cookie jars are the most commonly found pieces — and marked examples are rare. Blue is the most popular color.

For many years the Marshall Pottery of Marshall, Texas, has offered for commercial distribution "hand thrown" stoneware with blue sponge decoration or other blue decoration. This ware is often mistaken for the earlier pieces produced during the last century — because of its quality, and the fact that many of the first pieces produced by the Marshall Pottery were unmarked. Items made today are well marked in blue "Marshall Pottery, Marshall, Texas," and frequently the decorator's name is included. Items decorated by Kay Butler (deceased), are especially collectible.

Photographs: Olin and Ruby Fisher

Chapter IV
OTHER GLASS

BOHEMIAN GLASS

Bohemian glass is named for its country of origin. It is a two-layered glass, with the top layer always colored, while the inside layer is clear. Designs were cut into the colored layer, allowing the clear glass to show. This ware has been produced in black, blue, green, yellow, amber and ruby red, with the latter enjoying the greatest popularity among collectors.

New ruby and amber Bohemian glass has been produced in Czechoslovakia, West Germany and Poland in the stag or hunting scenes, the Vintage or Grapevine pattern, in addition to butterfly and floral designs.

Because the shapes being made today resemble those of original pieces so closely, the major difference between an early piece and a reproduction is in the quality of the workmanship and the absence of the usual recognizable signs of age.

The following new Bohemian pieces are being produced in RUBY or AMBER.

Bell, 5½" high
Bell

Bud Vase, 4¼" high
Butter Dish, Covered, 7¼" diam.
Candlesticks
Candy Boxes, 6½" diam.
Castor Bottles
Clarets
Cordials
Cordial Sets, 7 pc.
Cruets, 6"
Decanters, 16"
Epergne, 16"
Flip Vase, 10"
Glasses, Wine
Goblets
Liquor Set, 7 pc.
Lustres, 12"
Pitcher, 7½"
Roemers
Sherry
Sugar and Creamers, Covered
Tumbler, Water, 4"
Vases, 6", 6½", 8", 10", 13"
Wine Sets, 7 pc.

NEW BOHEMIAN GLASS

NEW BOHEMIAN SYRUP

88

CARNIVAL GLASS

The original Carnival glass era was from around 1900 to 1930. This ware was produced in quantities by the Northwood Glass Company of Martin's Ferry, Ohio; Imperial Glass Company, Bellaire, Ohio; Fenton Art Glass Company, Williamstown, West Virginia, and others.

Carnival glass is a type of pressed glass, with a metallic sheen and shifting rainbow hues. It is a lowcost version of the expensive Tiffany type iridescent glassware which was blown, not machine molded. Collectors refer to the glass as "Carnival" because it was given away at fairs and carnivals.

The task of identifying early Carnival is rather difficult at times, as it isn't unusual to find patterns so similar to each other that the variations are very slight. Over two hundred patterns are known to have been made, and it should be realized that virtually all of the molds used to produce the fine old Carnival still exist. However, only a few pieces are marked with an impressed mark that was molded into the glass. Those marks most often found are the letter "N" or "N" within a circle, used by the Northwood Glass Company.

Production of Imperial's pressed colored crystal with a lustrous finish began about 1910. The early ware was never marked with the overlapping "IG" cipher (impressed) found on their reissues. This particular mark wasn't adopted by the Imperial Glass Company until 1949, and appears on practically all of their production.

Many early reproductions of Carnival Glass were produced in England and Italy—and these pieces are easily detected by knowledgeable collectors, as the iridescent coloring (dull smoky color) doesn't compare to that of the original Carnival glass. The pieces produced in Italy were made in marigold and purple, and items made in England are made in purple, marigold and green.

The first commercial Carnival pieces to be produced in the United States for approximately 35 years were grape goblets, made by Imperial Glass Company in 1961. In January, 1965, Imperial swung out with a major line of 70 different pieces offered both in marigold and bluish purple. The list included 7 bowls, 8 covered boxes, 16 vases, jars, a basket, swan, decanter, 7-piece water sets, wine sets, punch set, etc. These first pieces were weighty, and the color was poor. In addition, a stipple finish was added to many of these pieces, which is not found on the originals. A year later, in January, 1966, Imperial moved into the rare and prized carnival field by marketing reproduced plates (Nuart, Homestead and Double Rose), toothpick holders, grape candlesticks and the zippered-look lamp. And in January, 1968, they added Red Carnival to their line, calling it Sunset Ruby. The quality of the new reproduced Carnival glass made by Imperial has improved, and it is becoming more and more collectible.

Other known glass firms producing new Carnival pieces are: Jeannette Glass Company; West Virginia Glass Specialty Company; St. Clair Glass Works; Fenton Art Glass Co.; and R. E. Hansen, Mackinaw, Michigan.

Two very famous early American patterns now being reproduced in Cobalt Blue, White, Marigold, Ice Blue Carnival and Amberina.

NEW CARNIVAL PIECES
by Imperial Glass Corp., Bellaire, Ohio

"Swung" Vase   "Swung" Vase   8½" Drama Vase   10" Vase   10" Vase   9" Bowl

3½" Candleholder   11½" 3 Toed Bowl   8" 3 Toed Bowl   3½" Candleholder

7¾" Tall Compote

9½" Tall Basket   5½" Hdld. Nappy   13 oz. Tankard Mug

4 pc. Toothpick Set

Butter and Cover   Box and Cover   4 Toed Jar and Cover   Ftd. Jar and Cover   Covered Jar

90

NEW CARNIVAL GLASS
by Imperial Glass Corp.

10 oz. Goblet

6 oz. Sherbert

3 oz. Wine

6 oz. Ftd. Juice

Egg Cup/Juice

12 oz. Tumbler

7½" Plate

Ftd. Sugar and Cream Set

Salt and Pepper Set

Cruet and Stopper

½ lb. Butter and Cover

Cup and Saucer

Bud Vase

4¾" Cr. Bowl

4½" Bowl

6" Handled Pickle Tray

1 Pint Pitcher

Salt and Pepper

"Spoonholder"
Sugar and Cover

Cream Pitcher

Sugar and Cream Set

Sugar and Cream Set

10½" Plate, Mum

10½" Plate, Homestead

10½" Plate, Rose

NEW CARNIVAL GLASS
by Imperial Glass Corp.

10" Vase

6" Vase

6¼" Vase

8½" Tricorn Vase

9½" Vase

"Cockerel"
Box and Cover

"Lion"
Box and Cover

Box and Cover

5" 4 Toed Vase

6½" Compote

8" Swan

8½" Footed Bowl

8" "Windmill"
Bowl, Crimped

11½" Salad Bowl

3 oz. Wine
Decanter and Stopper

Ftd. Wine
Decanter and Stopper

17" Lamp

NEW CARNIVAL GLASS
by Imperial Glass Corp.

9 oz. Tumbler   3 pint Pitcher

9 oz. Tumbler   3 pint Pitcher

9 oz. Tumbler   3 pint Pitcher

10 oz. Tumbler   3 pint Pitcher

15 pc. Punch Set

The heavy opalesence on this piece gives it a very "new" look. Its base color ranges from red at the top to amber at the base, with red streaks.

New Red Carnival Glass made by Imperial Glass Corporation, Bellaire, Ohio. Regardless of what iridescence has been applied to the surface, a genuine piece of red Carnival Glass, has a pure base color of "red" glass.

REPRODUCTIONS

ROW 1: Caramel Slag Tumbler (in the Holly Amber pattern)
ROW 2: Argonaut Shell Custard Bowl
ROW 3: Custard Toothpick, Kingfisher Pattern
            Custard Toothpick, Fan and Feather Pattern
ROW 4: Custard Toothpick, Holly Pattern
            Small Argonaut Shell Custard Bowl

95

CUSTARD GLASS

Custard Glass was manufactured in the United States for a period of about 30 years (1885-1915). Although Harry Northwood was the first and largest manufacturer of custard glass, it was also produced by Heisey Glass Company, Diamond Glass Company, Fenton Art Glass Company, and a number of others. Northwood designed, manufactured, and distributed his ware through various companies with which he was connected. Some of his pieces are marked on the bottom of the base with the word "Northwood" in script, or with an underscored "N" within a circle.

The name Custard Glass is derived from its "custard yellow" color, which may shade light yellow or ivory to light green glass that is opaque to opalescent. Most pieces of custard glass have a fiery opalescence when held up to an ordinary light. Both the color and the glow of this ware comes from the use of uranium salts in the glass. It is generally a "heavy" type glass, and was made in approximately 85 different patterns. It was manufactured primarily into table settings, berry sets, water sets, and other table and serving pieces. The majority of the old pieces were hand decorated with much gold decoration, especially on the feet or base.

The demand for custard glass has never been greater than at the present time. So, with prices soaring, new custard in the old formula, and from some of the old molds, was inevitable.

On January 6-7, 1969, the St. Clair Glass Works of Elwood, Indiana, produced four custard glass toothpick holders. The patterns were: Inverted Fan and Feather (Northwood); Kingfisher (Canton Glass Company, Marion, Indiana); Holly Band; and Indian Chief, both Greentown patterns. The quality of this new glass is very good,

showing much fiery opalescence. Three of the St. Clair toothpicks are pictured on page 103. Note how authentic the Inverted Fan and Feather example appears. Like other decorated custard pieces shown, it was decorated and fired after leaving the factory.

Next came a variety of novelty custard glass pieces by the Crystal Art Glass Company of Cambridge, Ohio, owned by Elizabeth Degenhart. Most of these pieces (bird salts, hands, covered hen, hats, miniature slipper, etc.), were sold to gift shops, and have not caused any great problem for collectors.

Then came the major production, creating much excitement for custard collectors. The Fenton Art Glass Company, made for the L. G. Wright Glass Company, numerous pieces of new custard glass bearing the old Northwood mark (underscored "N" within a circle). The color is creamy to light ivory, resembling that of the old Ivorina Verde custard glass.

Since the American Carnival Glass Assn., Washington, D. C., bought the mold rights and holds rights to the use of this Northwood mark, it was changed. A line was placed to the left of the "N", making it into a wobbly "W". Literally hundreds of pieces were marketed before the correction was made—and these will be confusing collectors for generations.

It should also be noted here, that already pieces of this glass are showing up "minus" the tiny angular line. When it has been removed (ground off), there will be an obvious dull spot on the surface of the glass.

The simplest method of differentiating the new custard glass from the old is its weight (lighter) and thin appearance.

New Decorated Custard Glass Tumblers bearing early Northwood mark. As expected, the tumblers have already become very collectible. Later examples are marked with the wobbly "W".

Cosmos Pattern   Grape and Daisy Pattern   Grape Pattern

NEW CUSTARD GLASS PIECES

Listed below are the new Custard glass pieces, known to have been produced up to the present time. When the letter "D" follows the name of a piece of glass, it indicates that the particular piece can also be purchased "decorated."

Argonaut Shell Covered Butter
Argonaut Shell Compote (small)
5″ Argonaut Shell Oval Bowl
11″ Argonaut Shell Bowl
Argonaut Shell Sugar and Creamer
Argonaut Shell Salt and Pepper
Argonaut Shell Toothpick
Argonaut Shell Tumbler
Beaded Shell Mug
6″ Cherry Scroll Compote
Cherry Creamer
Cherry Sugar
Cherry Toothpick
7″ Cosmos Bowl (D)
9″ Cosmos Plate (D)
Cosmos Tumbler (D)
Daisy and Button Kitten Slipper
Daisy and Button Medium Slipper
Fish Mug
Grape and Daisy Tumbler (D)

10½″ Grape and Fruit Bowl, Round (D)
12″ Grape and Fruit Bowl, Crimped (D)
14″ Grape and Fruit Plate (D)
Grape Tumbler (D)
7″ Hen on Nest
5″ Hen on Nest
Holly Band Toothpick
10″ Holly Bowl
12″ Holly Plate
Indian Chief Toothpick
Inverted Fan and Feather Toothpick
Kingfisher Toothpick
Kitten Slipper
5″ Owl on Nest
11″ Peacock Bowl, Crimped
12″ Peacock Plate
Plain Cream Pitcher, Tankard (D)
Plain Milk Pitcher, Tankard (D)
S Cup
S Toothpick
6″ Twig Crimped Nappy (D)
6″ Twig Plate (D)
7″ Twig Plate (D)
Wheat Tumbler

7″ Custard
Hen on Nest

11″ Custard
Argonaut Shell Bowl

5″ Custard
Argonaut Shell Oval Bowl

Undecorated Custard
Glass Milk Pitcher

10″ Holly
Custard Plate

Custard Cream Pitcher
with Moss Ross
Decoration

Custard Milk Pitcher
with Rose Vine Decoration

CUT GLASS

Cut glass with its deeply cut designs and intricate patterns, has been produced for centuries. The earliest cut glass made in the United States was probably manufactured during the last half of the eighteenth century by the Stiegel glass factory in Manheim, Pennsylvania. By the early 1800's, numerous American factories were making cut glasswares.

Research in recent years has produced a generally accepted system of dating American glass; however, these dates can only be accepted as outlines, because the styles always carried past influences with them.

The Early American Period dates from 1771-1830, the Middle Period from 1830-1880, and the Brilliant Period from 1880-1915. The majority of the cut glass offered for sale today dates from the Brilliant Period. These pieces were elaborately cut and costly when new. Cut glass was made in full sets for the table, and these pieces were used to serve any food that was not heated.

Numerous pieces of cut glass were marked (acid-etched) with the maker's name or trademark.

The new pieces of cut glass being sold today were produced in Germany, Italy, Poland and Czechoslovakia. The early examples were easily recognized, because portions of the cut detail work were poorly polished, and had a frosted appearance, whereas an old piece of cut glass was polished to perfection, and cuttings were deep and sharp. In addition, many of the early reproductions had a cloudy or "murky" appearance. The quality of the cut glass has improved during the last few years, making collecting a challenge for the amateur. However, reproductions still can be detected, as the rims of bowls are cut differently than the early ones; pitchers, tumblers and vases have extremely thick bases; and practically every piece of the new cut glass is very thick and heavy. The most frequent patterns found in the new glass are: pineapple, fan, pinwheel, and feather.

Three pieces of early cut glass of the Brilliant Period (1880-1915)

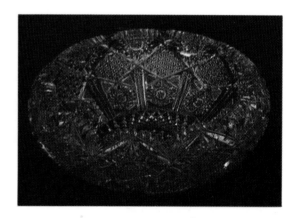

LACY SANDWICH GLASS

One of the most interesting and enduring pages from America's past is Sandwich Glass. Made at the famous Boston and Sandwich Glass Company, in the quaint Massachusetts town of Sandwich, the glass flourished from the years 1825 to 1888 throughout New England and America. After the factory closed in 1888 Sandwich Glass soon disappeared from practical table use, and began to appear more and more on collectors' shelves.

Despite the popularity of Sandwich Glass, little is known of its founder and guiding spirit, Deming Jarves. It is believed that he was born in Boston in 1791, the son of a well-to-do English immigrant, John Jack Jarves, who settled in New England in 1787. According to authorities in the field, it was Deming Jarves who acquired the original factory site in Sandwich and who raised the necessary capital. He also personally selected his aides, and hired the workers. The plant prospered immediately, and the tradition of Sandwich Glass was born.

The Sandwich glass house turned out hundreds of designs, in plain and figured patterns, and in colors and crystal, so that no one could be considered entirely typical, but one of the characteristic and popular treatments was the one known as "lace glass."

What made this glass so popular and unique?

Perhaps it was its lacy loveliness, magnificent intricate designs and glowing colors, combined with solid old New England practicality. The variety and multitude of designs and patterns produced by the company during its sixty years is a tribute to its greatness.

Today, a well-known glass company, Colony, is authentically reproducing Sandwich Glass in a wide range of serving pieces and accessories, with all the exquisite attributes and character of the original pieces, and colorful cup plates are being produced by Imperial Glass Company, Bellaire, Ohio.

It is a very simple matter to detect new Lacy Sandwich pieces, as the copies are lighter in weight; the surface of the glass is very glossy, whereas the early pieces have acquired a soft dull appearance with age; the finely raised dots (stippled background) on the underside of the glass are almost needle sharp, whereas on the original pieces the tiny raised dots of glass are smooth and rounded; and the new lacy pieces do not have a clear bell tone when tapped—you hear a dead thud one soon learns to associate with new glass.

It should be noted here that lacy glass was not made in complete sets of tableware as was the later pattern glass.

An American Heritage, Sandwich Glass was first made in 1825. Today, Colony reproduces the Star and Scroll Pattern with all the character and feeling of the original pieces.

99

2 pc. Cheese/Cracker
12" 2 Handled Plate
Covered Butter

Cup
Saucer
8" Salad Plate

SLAG OR MARBLE GLASS

The original name for this glass was "Mosaic," but for many years collectors have called it "Marble Glass" and "Slag Glass." Challinor, Taylor and Company of Tarentum, Pennsylvania, was the largest producer of this ware, and in the 1880's they advertised it as their "Mosaic Glass." The company produced a variety of pieces, including plates, bowls, covered novelty dishes, etc., mostly in a mottled purple and white variety.

A considerable quantity of fine pieces were produced in England, and many examples bear the English Registry mark on the bottom, or a peacock—a trademark of the Sowerly Glass Works of England.

The quality of Slag varies, but there appears to be three distinct types. The first is the open mix, where there is a definite line between the white and the color used. Actually it appears that the white mixture simply has not adhered properly to the colored mixture. Second is the fused mix, which has been well blended, thus showing a distinction of both the color and white, but not in separate masses. Third is the over mixed type, where white shows only occasionally.

The various slag mixtures to be found are: purple, red, pink, butterscotch, turqouise blue, orange, green and caramel.

A variety of attractive new Slag pieces have been produced by the Imperial Glass Company. The colors are purple, butterscotch (listed as "Caramel" in their catalogue), and red (listed as "End-O'Day" Ruby). Fortunately for collectors,

there are variations in patterns and shapes, which help identify this new ware from original pieces, as some pieces are not marked with the entwined "I G." The simplest way to distinguish a new piece from an old one is texture, as the new glass has a very slick, oily surface; whereas the early pieces feel dry and have acquired a soft worn appearance from usage. It will be of interest to note that all new Slag pieces made by Imperial are illustrated in this chapter. However, some of the caramel and purple slag pieces do not bear their identifying trademark, "I. G." Unfortunately, many collectors will probably end up with one of these reproductions—sooner or later.

Pink Slag, which shades from soft pink to creamy white, is attributed to the Indiana Tumbler and Goblet Company, Greentown, Indiana. Only a small quantity was produced in the Inverted Fan and Feather pattern—and these pieces are beautiful, rare, and expensive when found.

The only reproductions in Pink Slag known to me at this writing is a toothpick holder (made by St. Clair Glass Works in 1969), and tumbler, which was produced about six years ago. In this instance it is easy for the collector to identify the spurious as the coloring is exceedingly poor (dark, murky pink, shading to tan).

Caramel Slag was originally known as "Chocolate Glass." It was originated by Jacob Rosenthal, and manufactured at the Indiana Tumbler and Goblet Company, between November, 1900, and June 1903, when the factory was destroyed by fire. In 1912 a few pieces of this glass were produced by the Fenton Art Glass Company, then dropped. All Caramel Slag has a rich coffee appearance, with considerable variation in coloring which is primarily caused by the thickness of the glass. It can shade from a rich creamed coffee color to chocolate tones.

Collection: Mr. and Mrs. Harold Burns
Caramel and Purple Slag Toothpick Holders

100

NEW PURPLE

SLAG GLASS

by Imperial Glass Corporation
Bellaire, Ohio

Pokal

12 oz. Goblet

Goblet

6¼" Compote

6" Compote

7" 4 Toed Compote

"Heart Leaf"
Covered Box

6" Covered Bowl

Box and Cover

"Flat Iron"
Box and Cover

4 Toed Jar and Cover

"Lion"
Box and Cover

"Rooster"
Box and Cover

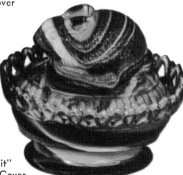

"Rabbit"
Box and Cover

101

"END O'DAY" RUBY (Red Slag)
Available in Glossy Finish and Satin Finish
Produced by Imperial Glass Corp., Bellaire, Ohio

9" Celery Vase   9½" Basket   7" Compote   5" Dolphin Candleholder   7" Dolphin Compote

Covered Jar   Covered Candy   Ftd. Bowl and Cover   Ftd. Oval Compote

5½" Covered Jar   Covered Candy   7½" Shell Tray   6" Vase   1 pint Pitcher

Sugar and Cream Set   Cruet and Stopper   8" Crimped Bowl   7½" Bowl

CASTER BOTTLES, Clear "Grape" pattern, five-bottle or six-bottle sets. (A. A. Importing Co., Inc.)

CASTER BOTTLES, Clear "Fern" pattern, five-bottle or six-bottle sets. (A. A. Importing Co., Inc.)

CASTER BOTTLES, Blue Overlay, "Rose" cutting, five-bottle and six-bottle sets. (A. A. Importing Co., Inc.)

CASTER BOTTLES, Clear "Wreath" pattern, five-bottle set. (A. A. Importing Co., Inc.)

CASTER BOTTLES, Inverted Thumbprint pattern, Cranberry five-bottle set. (A. A. Importing, Inc.)

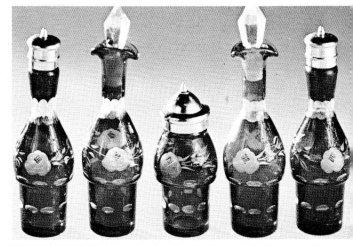

CASTER BOTTLES, Ruby Overlay, five-bottle or six-bottle sets. (A. A. Importing Co., Inc.)

Chapter V
MILK GLASS

MILK GLASS By Westmoreland

Of ancient origin, milk glass was revived in the 1700's by the English glassmakers in an effort to compete with porcelain. It is an opaque pressed glassware, usually of milk-white color, although green amethyst, black and shades of blue were made. Milk glass was heavily produced in the United States during the 1880's, often pressed in the same molds used for clear pattern glass.

Since the 1930's milk glass has been widely reproduced. Some of the new pieces have been made so skillfully that only the most experienced collectors can detect them, while others are very poor examples and can be easily recognized. Tex-

ture and weight play an important part in distinguishing between the early pieces of milk glass and the contemporary examples. An old piece is heavier, its texture is less oily and, from usage, it has lost much of its surface gloss. In addition, some of the early pieces have a rough spot on the foot of the glass which resembles the letter "C". This mark was formed in the molding and cannot be found on a reproduced piece of milk glass.

All of the Westmoreland reproductions illustrated in this chapter are marked on the base with the overlapping letters "W G."

Reproduced Milk Glass in "Old Quilt" Pattern: made by Westmoreland Glass Co.

3½" Box Square and Cover

Cheese

Compote Low Foot

Sweetmeat

NEW MILK GLASS
MADE BY JOHN E. KEMPLE GLASS WORKS, KENOVA, WEST VIRGINIA

Kemple Reproductions are made in the original molds. Whenever the design will allow, the Kemple factory pieces have the letter "K" on the bottom of each piece— thereby distinguishing them as reproductions.

EARLY MILK GLASS PIECES

Atterbury Owl, White Milk Glass. Courtesy of The Henry Ford Museum, Dearborn, Michigan.

Hen on Nest Dish, Blue Milk Glass body with White Head. Courtesy of The Henry Ford Museum, Dearborn, Michigan.

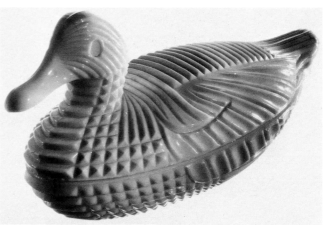

Atterbury Duck, White Milk Glass. Courtesy of The Henry Ford Museum, Dearborn, Michigan.

"Double Hands with Grapes." Authentic reproduction of an old 1880 original, often referred to as "Queen Victoria's Hands."

"Mother Eagle and Young," with Glass Eyes. 6 inches high. Authentic reproduction of a rare, hard-to-find original of Mother Eagle with spread wings protecting her young. Hand painted.

Basket and Cover, Wicker. This milk glass basket is 5¼ inches high by 5 inches long. Handle forms part of the cover. Authentic reproduction of old original.

Love Birds Covered Dish, 6½ inches by 5¼ inches high. An authentic reproduction of an original. Design on outside is repeated on inside of cover.

10″/15-pc. Punch Set. Consists of 5-quart punch bowl, pedestal, twelve punch cups and ladle. Fruit design in *bas-relief* on both bowl and cups. Made from an old Westmoreland mold.

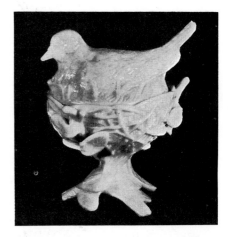

"Robin on Nest" Covered Dish. 6¼ inches high. An authentic handmade reproduction. Nest is formed of entwined twigs and leaves. Also made in Antique Blue Glass.

14″/15-pc. Punch Set, "Old Quilt" Pattern. Consists of 8-quart, bell-shape punch bowl, pedestal, ladle, and 12 matching punch cups.

15″ Punch Set, Fifteen-piece. Consists of large, 2¼-gallon punch bowl, pedestal, ladle, and twelve matching punch cups. A set reminiscent of late Victorian period. Also made in Crystal.

9″ Bowl, Bell, Footed, "Doric Border." Bowl is 7½ inches high. A representative piece in early American milk glass which Westmoreland has been making for three generations.

8" Plate, "Forget-me-not" Border. Also in an 11" size.

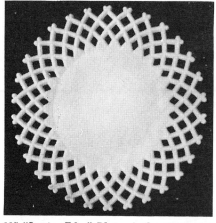

11" "Lattice Edge" Plate. Authentic reproduction of the "open-end" lattice original.

7" "Fleur-de-lis" Milk Glass Plate. An authentic reproduction of a popular old original.

7" Plate, "Three Kittens." An authentic reproduction of very popular novelty plate of the late 1800's.

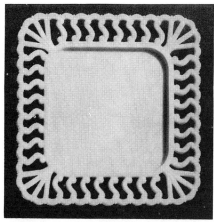

8½" Plate, "Square 'S'" Border. Originals have long been a collector's item.

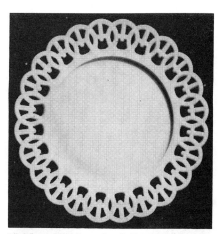

9" Plate, "Wicker-edge," Round. Authentic reproduction of a much sought after 1880 original.

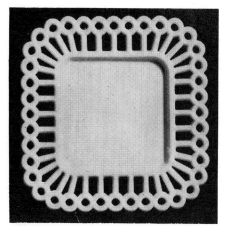

8¼" Plate, "Square Peg Border."

8" Plate, "Heart" Shape. Twenty small hearts form the border of the reproduction of this deep depressed center plate.

8" Plate, "Top Border." A Westmoreland original.

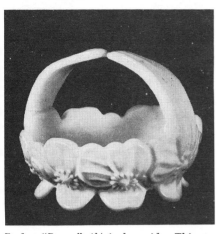

Basket, "Pansy." 4½ inches wide. This attractive little dish is a Westmoreland perrennial favorite. One of the oldest and most popular small items. Also made in Antique Blue Glass and Crystal, as well as Decorated.

6½" Compote and Cover. Footed, "Sawtooth." Authentic reproduction of one of the earliest milk glass patterns.
AT RIGHT: *6½" Covered dish, "Sawtooth."* 5 inches high.

9" Bowl and Cover, Footed, "Sawtooth." 14 inches in height. Authentic handmade reproduction of a cherished, old 1859 original.

"Mother Eagle with Young," Oval Bowl. Decorated in color. Has glass eyes.

5½" Sleigh Bowl with Santa Claus Cover in plain milk glass. This covered bowl is 4½ inches high by 5½ inches long.
5½" Sleigh Bowl, only, plain milk glass. Both items may be found decorated.

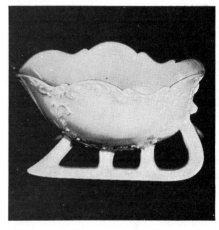

Sleigh Bowl, Large, plain or decorated.

Plate, "Fleur de lis." With hand painted Parakeet.

"Fleur de lis," with hand plainted Parakeet.

8½" dec. Bowl, Round, "Lattice Edge." Hand painted flower cluster.
11" Bowl, Flared, "Lattice Edge." With hand painted flower cluster, same hand painted design on both. These are also made without decoration.

111

6" Bowl and Cover, "Shell." An attractive three-footed, small bowl, with three dolphin-like legs. Shell motif on bowl and cover is the dominant pattern. Also made in "Golden Sunset" Crystal.

3ftd. Candy Jar and Cover, Ribbed. Six inches high. One of the early reproductions made by Westmoreland.

Candy Jar and Cover, "Ball and Swirl." Footed, 7 inches high. Also made in "Golden Sunset" Crystal.

Hand and Dove on Oblong, Footed Bowl. Hand holding Dove has glass jewel simulating precious stone. Dove has glass eye. This bowl is 5 inches by 8 inches; 5 inches high.

7" Plate. "Three Owls," Looped Border. An authentic reproduction of an old souvenir plate, with hand painted owls. This plate is also made in plain milk glass without decoration.

6" Bonbon, "Leaf," with hand painted "Roses and Bows" Design.

7½" 2hld. Cookie Jar and Cover, "Cherry" Pattern. Bright red cherries decorate this handled, covered bowl; also in plain milk glass, without decoration.

Sugar and Cream Set, "Cherry" Pattern. Handled sugar is 3¼" inches high, matching creamer is 3¾ inches high. Also plain, without decoration.

5½" Honey and Cover, Footed, "Cherry" Pattern. Hand painted cherries and leaves on cover. Also made in plain milk glass.

Fox with Glass Eyes, on 8″ Footed Oval Bowl. This piece is 6½ inches high by 8 inches long. Authentic reproduction of an old original.

Lion on 8″ Oval Lacy-Edge Bowl. Lion has glass eyes. This piece, 6 inches tall, is reproduced from an authentic, late 1800 original.

Cat on Lacy-Edge, Oblong, Footed, Bowl. Cat has glass eyes. The bowl measures 5″ by 8″, with cover, the piece is 6½″ high. Reproduced from a popular old milk glass original.

Rabbit Covered Dish (with or without pink eyes and ears). Octagonal, ribbed, bottom is 5½ inches long. This *"Mule-eared Rabbit"* is made from a very old Westmoreland mold.

Swan with raised wings on lacy-edge dish 6 inches by 9½ inches. Authentic reproduction of milk glass Swan made in the late 1880's.

Large Rooster, plain Milk Glass, with glass eyes. 8″ Lacy-Edge, Oval Bowl. Also with red decorated comb.

Large Rabbit, with Decorated Eggs and Grass. 7 inches wide by 5 inches high. Also in plain milk glass, or *with Painted Eyes and Mouth.* White eggs.

8″ Large Rabbit, without decoration. 8″ Oblong, Lacy-Edge, Footed Bowl. Also in plain milk glass.

Large Duck, 8½″ long. Authentic Westmoreland reproduction of duck with glass eyes, on straight edge, oval, milk glass bottom.

LEFT: *10" "Wedding Bowl" and Cover in plain milk glass.*
RIGHT: *8" "Wedding Bowl" and Cover in plain milk glass. Hand painted "Wedding Bowls" also being made.*

14" Banana Bowl, Square, Footed, "Ring and Petal" Border. 9½ inches high.

11" Cake Salver, Square, Footed, "Ring and Petal" Border. 4½ inches high.

10" Bowl, Cupped, Footed, "Lattice-Edge."

11" Bell Bowl, Footed, "Lattice-Edge."

12" Bowl, Banana, Footed, "Lattice-Edge." It stands 8½ inches high

11" Salver, Cake, Footed, "Lattice-Edge." This piece is 5 inches high.

4" Candlesticks, "Lattice-Edge" Pattern.

TOP: *5x8" Lacy-Edge Oblong Bowl, "Dancing Sailors." 8 inches by 5 inches. Authentic copy of old original.*
BOTTOM: *8" Bowl, Oval, Footed, "Dancing Sailors." 3½ inches high.*

AUTHENTIC REPRODUCTIONS OF "RING AND PETAL" PATTERN by Westmoreland

Westmoreland's handmade reproductions of the old *"Ring and Petal"* Border Pattern. Reproductions are from old originals.

TOP ROW: *7" Bowl, Square, Footed, "Ring and Petal."* 5 inches high.
8" Plate, "Ring and Petal." Border has

deep depressed center.
8½" Bowl, Round, Footed, "Ring and Petal" Border. 4½ inches high.

CENTER ROW: *3½" Candlesticks, "Ring and Petal" Border.*
11" Square Bowl, "Ring and Petal" Border. Without foot.

BOTTOM ROW: *10" Bowl, Flared, Low Foot, "Ring and Petal" Border.* Measures 3½ inches high.
12" Salver, Cake, Low Foot, "Ring and Petal" Border. Measures 1¾ inches high. All *"Ring and Petal"* items are authentic handmade reproductions.

12" Bowl, Bell, Footed, "Ring and Petal" Border.

Cheese and Cover, "Ring and Petal" Border Plate with "American Hobnail Cover.

115

8½" Bowl, Straight Edge, Footed, "Dancing Sailors" Pattern.

7¼" Bowl, Round, Footed, "Dancing Sailors Pattern. Authentic Reproduction.

9" Bowl, Square, "Dancing Sailors." An authentic reproduction of a rare old original. Pattern derives its name from the similarity in appearance of border design to paper cut-outs of little dancing sailors.

9" Bowl, Bell, Footed, "Dancing Sailors."

TOP: *Straight-edge Oval Bowl.* Authentic handmade milk glass reproduction. 10" by 7¾".
BOTTOM: *Lacy-Edge, Oval Bowl.* Sides are turned up. Bowl is 6¼" wide.

11½" Bowl, Oval, Footed, "Lotus" Pattern. Made from a very old mold.

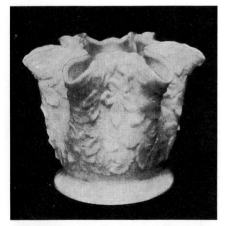

8" Bowl, Six Point, "Maple Leaf." All over "Leaf" Pattern, 6 inch high. Made from a very old mold.

7½" Bowl, Round, Rippled Edge, Footed, "Maple Leaf." 4" high bowl.

9" Candlesticks, "Dolphin." A reproduction of one of the popular Sandwich *Dolphin originals.* There were many variations of this item made by early American glassmakers with the "Dolphin" motif.

NEW MILK GLASS PIECES by Westmoreland

12" Compote, Shell, "Dolphin." An authentic reproduction of a original.

Covered Dish, "Chick on Eggs." 6½ inches high. Chick's head with glass eyes, colored eggs on painted bowl. Also made with Painted Chick. Yellow head, and glass eyes; green grass.

Large Rooster, Decorated, Minorca, with glass eyes, on milk glass bottom.

Large Hen, Decorated Minorca.

Large Rooster, with red or plain Comb, and glass eyes, on 8" Lacy-Edge, Oval Bowl.

Large Hen, red or plain Comb. Milk Glass on 8" Lacy-Edge Oval Bowl bottom.

8½" Breakfast Plate, "Beaded-Edge." With Hand Painted, colored Leghorn Rooster decoration.

8½" Breakfast Plate, "Beaded-Edge." With Hand Painted Pair of Chicks. White and colored Leghorn Hens and Roosters, Rhode Island Red Hen and Rooster.

8" Breakfast Plate, "Beaded-Edge." With Hand Painted, colored Leghorn Hen decoration.

NEW MILK GLASS VASES AND PLANTER by Westmoreland

TOP ROW: *12" Vase, Hand Blown, "Paneled Grape."*
11½" Vase, Bell, Footed, "Paneled Grape.
9" Vase, Bell, "Old Quilt" Pattern.
9" Vase, Bell, Footed, "Ball and Swirl"
Pattern.
15" Vase, "Paneled Grape" Pattern.
Height varies on this vase.

SECOND ROW: *6½" Vase, Celery, "Old Quilt."*
9" Vase, Fan Shape, "Old Quilt."
6" Vase, Crimped, Footed, "Beaded Grape" Pattern.
5" x 9" Planter, Oblong, "Paneled Grape."
BOTTOM ROW: *9" Vase, Crimped, Footed, "Beaded Grape" Pattern.*

9" Vase, Bell, "Paneled Grape."
Vase, Bud, "Paneled Grape."
7" Vase, "Lily." Truly Exquisite.
Vase, Tall, Celery, "Paneled Grape" Pattern.
Vase, Crimped, Footed, "Paneled Grape" Pattern.

11" Plate with hand painted Wild Turkey, "Lattice Edge." The full set of Eight Game Birds consists of Wild Turkey, Bobwhite, Pheasant, Grouse, Snipe, Woodcock, Blue Jay and Redbird.

11" Plate with hand painted Bobwhite, "Lattice Edge." In natural colors. There are Eight Game Birds in the assortment.

11" Plate with hand painted Pheasant, "Lattice Edge."

11" Plate with hand painted cluster of Old Fashioned Flowers, "Lattice Edge."

11" Plate with hand painted Male Mallard Duck in flight. "Lattice Edge." Available in Male Mallard and Baby Mallard.

11" Plate with hand painted Female Mallard Duck in flight. "Lattice Edge.

11" Plate with hand painted Rose and Gold Leaves, "Lattice Edge." Plate has been called "The aristocrat of Milk Glass Plates."

7" Plate with hand applied Floral Decals, "Beaded Edge." Four designs: Columbine, Iris, Bluebell, and Daisy.

7" Plate with hand applied Decal of French, Watteau Scene, "Fleur-de-lis" Border.

NEW MILK GLASS PLATES by Westmoreland

8" Black Glass "Forget-me-not" Plate.

8" dec. Black Glass "Forget-me-not" Plate with hand painted white enamel scene of Girl with Dog.

8" dec. Black Glass "Forget-me-not" Plate with hand painted white enamel scene of Boy with Rake and Dog.

8" dec. Black Glass "Forget-me-not Plate with hand painted white enamel Running Buck.

8" dec. Black Glass "Forget-me-not Plate with hand painted white enamel scene of Girl in Swing.

8" dec. Black Glass "Forget-me-not Plate with hand painted white enamel scene of Boy Fishing.

8" dec. Black Glass "Forget-me-not Plate with hand painted white enamel scene of Standing Doe.

8" dec. Black Glass "Forget-me-not Plate with hand painted white enamel scene of Girl with Sled.

8" dec. Black Glass "Forget-me-not" Plate, hand painted white enamel scene of Boy Skating with Dog.

WESTMORELAND'S FAMOUS OLD MILK GLASS CHICKEN FAMILY

TOP ROW: *Large Hen with red comb.* 7½ inches long by 5¾ inches wide. *Standing Rooster with red comb, yellow feet.* 8½ inches tall. Also in "Minorca" decoration.

CENTER ROW: *Medium Hen with read comb.* 5½ x 4 inches. *Hen on Handled Basket,* 4 inches high. *Rooster on ribbed dish,* with decorated comb and eye. 5½ inches long.

BOTTOM ROW: *Small Hen, decorated comb.* 3 inches long. *Toy Chick, 2 inches long.* Toy chickens are made in 6 assorted colors.

NEW MILK GLASS by Westmoreland

Bud Vase   Bud Vase   4½" Candlestick   10" Wedding Bowl   9" Bowl and Cover, Ftd. Sq.   12½" Urn and Cover

Double Hands   Pansy Basket   5" Honey   6½" Oval Basket   4" Bowl and Cover, Square   4½" Puff Box   5 oz. Toilet Bottle

Covered Sugar   7" Compote and Cover   5" Bowl, Flared, Ftd.   8" Wedding Bowl   7" Bowl and Cover, Sq. Ftd.   9" Fan Vase

6¼" Candy Jar   3½" Square Box and Cover   4 pc. Dresser Set   6" Wedding Box   6" Vase, Crimped, Ftd.   6½" Celery Vase

122

Chapter VI
LAMPS

LAMPS

An old Victorian lamp adds immeasurable pleasure and beauty to interiors in our present design for living and, because of the great interest in and increasing demand for lamps, many types have been abundantly reproduced. As you collect lamps, keep in mind that there are the intentional fakes where "parts" have been specially treated to obtain the look of their counterparts to trap the unwary; there are reproductions that have been meticulously copied in the hope that it would require an expert to determine the difference between the spurious and the original; and there are the contemporary examples that look "too" new to be taken for authentic work but, in time, will confuse collectors.

With the coming of electricity, thousands of oil lamps found their way to the attic or basement or disappeared into barrels and boxes and for years lay domant. After the movie **Gone with the Wind,** these old Victorian lamps skyrocketed to popularity, and today collectors diligently search for original examples. Many of the early examples have been converted to electricity; however, more and more serious collectors are refraining from this practice in order to preserve the antiquity of the lamps.

The most discernible factors that identify a new lamp are the lack of natural wear marks on all parts, and the texture of the new glass shades, as well as decoration. Usually, a collector will only look at the base of a lamp which is obviously old and shows signs of wear. They never bother to examine closely the other parts.

Lamps selected to be included in this chapter are the examples which are causing the greatest confusion in the field today.

Baby Face
GONE WITH THE WIND
LAMP

Authentic Reproduction

Reproduction of a Lovely Victorian Hanging Fixture with prisms. AMBER, BLUE, GREEN, or RUBY. Approx. 25" overall length. 10" shade, with frosted chimney. Electrified with key in gallery. Available with, or without prisms.

Orchids and Blue Flowers, Green leaves on Pink background. (Reproduction)

COURTESY OF **W. N. de SHERBININ** PRODUCTS, Inc.

NEW HANGING LAMPS

Hanging Lamp with Brass Font and Dresden Shade with New England Aster Design.

Hanging Lamp with Brass Font and Dresden Melon Shade with Maple Leaf Design.

Hobnail Shade and Font with prisms and Brass hardware, Amber, Blue and Ruby.

New Early American and Victorian Bracket Lamps

Candy Stripe Gas Shade Holder with matching Font, Fenced Brass Holder. Blue Candy Stripe. Cranberry Stripe.

Petticoat Bracket Lamp in Amber, Blue, Green and Cranberry.

"NEW" LAMPS

New Cranberry IVT 19"
Lamp with 8" Shade.

Courtesy of B & P Lamp Supply
Company, McMinnville, Tennes-
see.

New 31" Maize Pattern
Lamp with 12" Shade.

126

Satin Glass Lamp

Reproduced Fairy Lamp. White Exterior, Peachblow Interior with Satin Finish.

Reproduced Hobnail Fairy Lamp: Colors: Amber, Blue, Green and Ruby.

NEW "GONE WITH THE WIND" LAMPS

Satin Glass Lamp

THREE COLORFUL EXAMPLES (24" diam.) OF THE NEW TIFFANY TYPE GLASS
HANGING SHADES, NOW BEING MARKETED

Wisteria Pattern

Cherry Pattern

Fruit and Bird Pattern

Tiffany Table Lamp with Daffodill Shade.
Courtesy of The Henry Ford Museum,
Dearborn, Michigan.

Parlor Lamp, Painted Wild Roses on Blue
Shade and Base—1875-1890. Courtesy
of The Henry Ford Museum, Dearborn,
Michigan.

Kerosene Hanging Lamp. Courtesy of
The Henry Ford Museum, Dearborn,
Michigan.

129

NEW HANGING LAMPS
Courtesy of B & P Lamp Supply Company
McMinnville, Tennessee

Chapter VII
PAPERWEIGHTS

PAPERWEIGHTS

Paperweights with their wondrously ornamental colored designs, are actually man-made jewels. They were built, rather than blown by a variety of processes. Venetian glass blowers made the first paperweights during the early nineteenth century and by 1820, they were being made in France at St. Louis. Around 1850 workmen skilled in paperweight techniques moved from Italy, France and England to the United States, and American glasshouses from New England south to Virginia began experimenting with paperweights. Although many American weights show a European influence because they were made by immigrant gaffers, they were never as brilliant as the weights produced in such French centers as Baccarat, Cristalleries de Saint Louis in Paris, Cristalleries et Verreries de Vianne (Cristal d'Albret), and the Clichy manufacturers in France.

Paperweights are categorized according to their diameters. The three categories that are accepted by scholars and collectors are the miniature (2-inch diameter or less), the standard (2- to 3½-inch diameter), and the magnum (over 3-inch diameter).

Although glasshouses in the east and midwest derived much of their inspiration from European designs, each glasshouse developed its own specialties. The most unusual and handsome weights were produced in the East Cambridge factory by Francois Pierre, who had supposedly been trained in the Baccarat factory. His blown apple and pear weights are treasured.

The New England Glass Company had molds for flowers, animals, letters, figures and stars which made up the decorative devices around which their weights were constructed. These could be combined for an almost-endless variety.

Many of the weights consisted of floral arrangements placed over a latticinio ground; these were known as Venetian. In later years the company made weights using pressed objects such as reclining dogs, turtles, and a miniature Plymouth Rock.

Modern paperweights are being made today in many countries. Some examples display the old techniques, while others have a contemporary look. Although comparatively few old paperweights were signed and dated, many of the modern ones are. Weights made in Sweden and the United States often are signed with the names of artist and glass factory and, occasionally, one is dated. Paperweights produced in the early 1900's by Louis Comfort Tiffany bear his name or his initials and, perhaps, the word Favrile.

With increasing prices and fine old paperweights becoming more difficult to find, it is extremely necessary for collectors to examine a weight before buying. Modern weights are much lighter than the early examples. A good paperweight was made from fine, clear glass and, if the glass was a good quality of lead glass, it was heavy. Many of the new weights have flaws in the glass, some are on the cloudy side and, like so much of the new glass being produced today, the new weights feel slick or greasy when touched. Most early weights were used and will have some sign of natural wear which removes a slight amount of surface gloss.

Pontil marks are also helpful in identifying weights. The modern ones being mass-produced today have ground flat bases (sometimes frosted), whereas good old weights have convex bottoms (slightly curved or rounded).

PAPERWEIGHTS

Courtesy of
Bergstrom Art Center & Museum
Neenah, Wisconsin

Courtesy of
Bergstrom Art Center & Museum
Neenah, Wisconsin

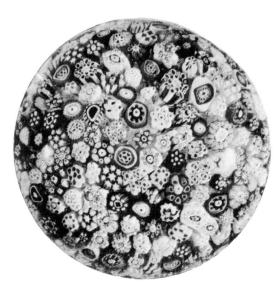

Courtesy of
Bergstrom Art Center & Museum
Neenah, Wisconsin

"NEW" PAPERWEIGHTS made by Pilgrim Glass Company

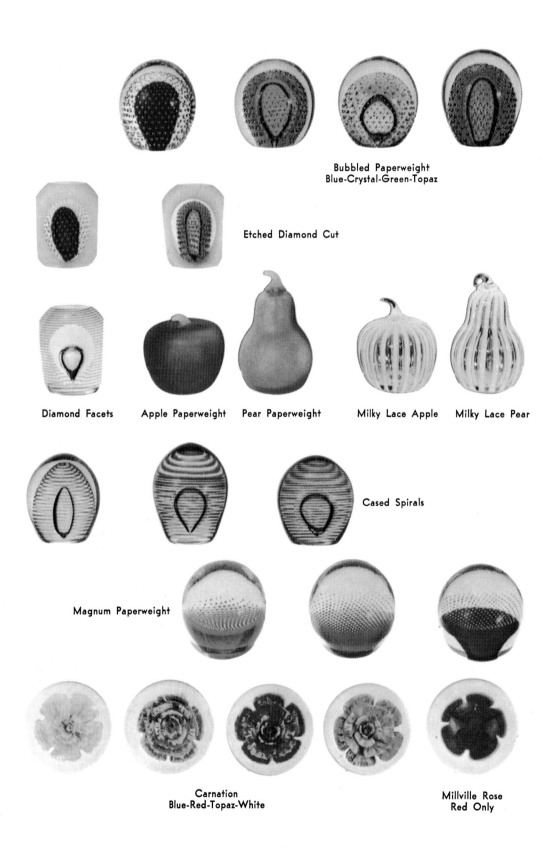

Bubbled Paperweight
Blue-Crystal-Green-Topaz

Etched Diamond Cut

Diamond Facets   Apple Paperweight   Pear Paperweight   Milky Lace Apple   Milky Lace Pear

Cased Spirals

Magnum Paperweight

Carnation
Blue-Red-Topaz-White

Millville Rose
Red Only

New Paperweights made by
John E. Kemple Glass Works, Kenova, West Virginia

136

Chapter VIII
FURNITURE

FURNITURE

There is a great deal of furniture made today that attempts in one degree or another to reproduce the styles of the past. Some pieces claim to be authentic reproductions, almost flaunting a pedigree; others, authentic adaptations; still others, interpretations of the past. To the amateur who loves and appreciates fine old furniture, but really doesn't know how to distinguish the difference between the old and the new, collecting often becomes a very bewildering and frustrating experience. The best reproductions are made by people with a thorough knowledge of antiques and their history, and most new pieces are as much like the originals as it is humanly possible to make them.

For judging antiques, then, a background is essential. There is no direct or sure method for the average person to follow in achieving expert proficiency in a short time; but like other fields of collecting, there are some pointers which should be observed and they are patina, normal signs of wear, construction, condition and types of woods. In addition, the more trips collectors can make to museums, the more good antique shows they can attend, and the more visits they make to shops of reliable dealers in fine antiques, the sharper their eyes will be in weeding out the reproduction, the adaptation, etc., because every old piece of furniture carries, plainly written over its various parts and surfaces, an accurate record of its age and treatment. When considering a piece of furniture, here are thirty pointers which can be helpful to the beginner.

1. Patina is the surface appearance that wood acquires through age and usage. This thin layer of tiny scratches, cuts, and bruises gives an old piece of furniture its mellow quality of color and texture—it cannot be imitated or hurried.

2. Despite the sophistication of modern furniture-making machinery, producers are unable to achieve finishes or carving that equal the work of artisans. The depth and the clarity of the carving on aged furniture will give a clue as to whether it has been done by hand or by machine. When a piece has been hand carved, the edges will be clean-cut, while machine work may be round, even splintery, at the edges, and careful examination will reveal whether a piece of decoration has been carved in or merely glued on.

3. When considering the authenticity of pieces of furniture, it is always wise to feel the exposed edges of table tops, drawer fronts, edges of drawers, and the outer corners of all square posts of tables and chairs. There should be a noticeable difference, as all exposed locations on early furniture will lack knife-like edges or sharp corners. Wear and usage have removed them. The only sharp edges found on aged furniture will be found only in places quite protected by their location.

4. Chairs will be worn where they should be worn. For instance, on tall four and five-slat-back chairs, the wear on the posts is usually more prominent where the shoulder blades and upper back of the occupant came into contact with them. The back section of the arm rail of a Windsor armchair is always more worn on the inside than the outside, as the rail never touched the wall or encountered much friction. And the finials of turned chairs nearly always show the results of friction, as most of the wear was directly at the back where they have rubbed or come into contact with the wall.

5. Look at the legs and feet on chairs for signs of wear. The front edge of feet is more rounded and worn than those on the back side, caused from being dragged on the floor. The area on feet that comes in contact with the floor will often be finely polished by wear, and frequently black in color. And, being close to the floor, chair legs, as well as table legs, will bear slight dents and bruises where they have been hit.

6. Chair rungs should always be considered when dating furniture. The lower ones in front will be worn practically flat from the rubbing of many pairs of shoes. The side chair rungs will also show wear, but the back rung will lack wear marks. In the same way, stretchers of a table will be worn, indicating years of use.

7. The edges of feet on chairs, tables, chests, beds, etc., often suffer decay from moisture, as many pieces were stored in basements, barns, etc.

8. Very wide boards were used before the true mass production of furniture began after the Civil War. In the case of tabletops, an old

wide board will have two characteristics indicating age. First, the boards will invariably warp to some extent. Second, over the years they will shrink, causing sprung hinges and splits in tabletops. And a table with a round top supported by a column, will measure less across the grain than it will the length of it.

9. The backboard on pieces of country furniture was usually left in the rough. Close inspection will reveal ridges and hollows left by the wide-bladed jackplain which was used until around 1835.

10. Drawers on old furniture are sure places to find signs of wear, even if the pieces came from a mansion and had perfect care. Fronts will be scratched, bruised or nicked, and many old drawers fit loose. Sometimes the sides of a drawer will be so worn that the drawer will tilt downward when half open. And it will be noteworthy to add that the interiors of drawers on early country furniture were usually never varnished, and their exterior bottom was left in a rough condition.

11. The dovetail joint, named for the shape of the flaring tenon, was used for joining sides, tops and bottoms of case pieces, and was always used in drawer construction. Very early pieces were joined with one large dovetail, from three to four inches wide, which fit into a corresponding open mortice. With the passing of time, three or five dovetails appeared on drawers, each cut by hand and the spacing and size was different, reflecting the individual cabinet-maker's preference. Evenly spaced machine-cut dovetails (eight or more small ones), appeared on early Victorian furniture.

12. Mortise and tenon joints on seventeenth and early eighteenth-century pieces have wide tenons (2 to 4 inches), and are fastened with wooden pegs driven into holes bored through the joint. Tenons became narrower after the introduction of glue—and frequently pinning was omitted.

13. Drawer runners should always be examined for signs of considerable wear from decades of friction.

14. Wood pegs on early furniture were usually made from hickory or ash. Some were oblong or square; none were perfectly round. Today, pegs are used as decorative notes in reproductions, and they are perfectly

round. An old peg will frequently project from the surface, while the round pegs on reproductions are cut off exactly flush with the surface.

15. Wood pins were hand-carved and many-sided. Some are oval, others are square and octagonal, but they're never round. Like pegs, a pin fitted into holes in two adjacent pieces of wood to hold them together.

16. Sawmarks are always a good indication of age and easy to identify. Most saws used by cabinetmakers were straight, hand-operated ones with coarse teeth, leaving a clear pattern of straight parallel scratches. The circular saw (buzz saw, always power driven) was not generally used in the United States until around the middle of the nineteenth century.

17. Serious collectors say they can smell old wood. It has a distinct "musty" odor.

18. Wood changes color slowly. A protected area will not darken as quickly as one that is exposed to light and air.

19. The hand-wrought nail (the oldest type) varies in size, and can be found on furniture made before 1815. Machine-made nails (sometimes square-headed) came into use around 1815 and are still being made and sold. Wire nails were not in general use until about 1875.

20. Wood screws were made by hand and used by early furniture makers. Threads were uneven, and the narrow slot in the head was usually off center. Blunt end machine-made screws date from 1815, and the pointed screw was produced around 1850.

21. All brasses, hinges and knobs have been reproduced so widely that they cannot always be considered when determining the age of furniture. However, it is possible to learn whether brass or copper hardware is what it may appear to be. If a magnet clings to the hardware, it is iron or steel that has been plated to resemble brass or copper.

22. Early glass used in cupboard doors is often wavy and bubbly and, occasionally, it will be slightly blue in color. Sheet window glass was in use by the middle of the Victorian era.

23. Wormholes, which many people look for and expect to find, are not an indi-

spensable sign of age. Unless man-made, wormholes are tiny, round, very sharp holes varying in sizes, rather than uniform, as when made by a shotgun. Furthermore, worms never expose their channel on the outside of a piece of wood. The holes that they make are merly entrances to their homes.

24. It is wise to learn the appearance of old wood. Frequently, new woods have been specially treated and handled to obtain the look of their counterparts. An artificially aged piece is different in color, with more orange or gray tones.

25. When gold trim is used, look for a rich undertone, rather than surface glitter. The early cabinetmakers applied real gold leaf over a red Spanish clay. Today, anodized metals are used and often the gold colored metal is applied over a layer of deep-pink paint, to give a reproduction the depth and color tone of an antique.

26. A piece of early furniture may have on its surfaces anywhere from one to a dozen coats of paint of various colors and, therefore, a small section of every surface of such a piece will exhibit, if scraped to the wood, the same colored layers of paint, each layer in its proper order.

27. Very thick old paint is extremely hard and brittle, and will shatter when hit with a hammer. When old paint is scraped with a knife, it comes off in tiny chips or powder, as the elasticity of the oil has been lost. New paint retains its elasticity for several years and, when scraped, is more likely to prove softer and less glasslike. When recently applied heavy paint is scraped, it will come off in strips and narrow ribbons. Patina of old painted pieces is darker and richer than that of new ones. This is especially apparent with old chairs and chests.

28. Be very cautious when an authentic piece of furniture is offered at extreme low price. It is strange, but true, that the unscrupulous seller seldom has the nerve or courage to ask a price which would be right for a genuine piece. Whenever you are asked $100 for something that is worth three times as much, use extreme caution.

29. Old furniture may ethically be restored to its original condition, which may include minor repairs, or the addition of a missing part. But when the buyer thinks that a piece is entirely original, it is always disappointing to discover even a minor replacement, or a camouflaged new part. So—by all means—examine old furniture before you buy.

There are many pieces of furniture marketed each year which have been constructed entirely from different pieces of old wood. This fakery is especially prevalent in the field of early pine pieces, such as dry sinks, cupboards, chests of drawers, blanket chests and cobbler's benches. In most instances, these fraudulent pieces are easily recognized—and spotting one is simply a matter of close observation. The biggest giveaway is empty nail holes in places where there was never any reason for nails in the construction of the piece. Frequently, these holes are filled with plastic wood. The uniformity in the color and texture of surfaces is also very important, because the exterior, as well as all interior parts, on an aged piece of furniture will exhibit the same consistency of color.

30. Finally, there are still many quality pieces of furniture for sale which are genuine, authentic, and right in every way. It is simply a matter of distinguishing the new from the old. Through actual experience, intensive study, together with common sense, a serious collector will develop an intuition—and this "sixth sense" will serve as a guide.

Reproductions that have been copied faithfully from early examples in museums and restorations are available today in the widest range. Amazingly enough, many collectors are unaware of their existence. Accurate as the current "furniture store" reproductions and adaptations may be, always remember they are factory-made. The original models were turned out individually, and these early pieces were made by hand in cabinet makers' shops until the 1830's and, in some instances, many years thereafter. So, the details of construction and carving on these new pieces appear quite different to the knowledgeable collector.

What has been chosen for mention in this chapter has been selected to give collectors some knowledge of what is currently being produced in this field.

Do-It-Yourself Products
Interest in Americana is at a high pitch today and, if Early American antiques were available and collectors could afford them, they would ob-

viously be their first choice. So, it isn't surprising that their second choice might be an exact copy of a museum piece.

The do-it-yourself products, so common today, were in use over two hundred years ago. Itinerant peddlers were selling unassembled chair parts, and were organizing "building bees" for farmers before 1800. Cohasset Colonials by Hagerty, Cohasset, Massachusetts, have revived a centuries-old custom—selling furniture in parts. These reproductions have been copied so accurately that museum officials recognize their faithfulness. All products are branded with the Hagerty hallmark, to attest their authenticity. It is, of course, a sad commentary upon human nature that there are some persons—happily in the minority—who are assembling these pieces (especially chairs), and who think nothing of removing the brand mark (by sanding), painting or abrading these pieces to simulate wear, and letting them pass themselves off as authentic antiques.

18th Century Reproductions

During the past several years Yale R. Burge has concentrated on exact replicas of antiques from private collections and museums. He obtains the rights to reproduce the piece or sometimes buys the original. Very often famous French cabinet makers are used to make the master models, then Burge's own American craftsmen produce the reproduction in his own New York workrooms. He personally supervises finishing of many of the items. He also chooses fabrics for upholstered pieces and has a penchant for color and pattern which he often purposefully contrasts to what is expected. His unique flair in upholstery of reproductions is in his use of unexpected silks, glove leathers, dress fabrics, tweeds, wools or whatever.

Mr. Burge formed his own firm to produce reproductions about 15 years ago. His first collection featured about 30 copies of antiques, and today there are several hundred different individual pieces reproduced by the Burge firm. One hallmark of the Burge reproductions is selectivity. Another is the acute attention to detail. Unlike ordinary reproductions, Burge reproduces many of his pieces exactly in both scale and carving, even simulating the finish of the carefully preserved antique which is the counterpart of the reproduction.

Burge has sought out "signed" pieces and pieces attributed to famous 18th century European craftsmen for his collection. I. Avisse, Georges Jacob, Henri Amand, I. B. Meunier, Jean Baptiste Tilliard, I. Boucault, Jean Laurent, P. Forget, Michael Cresson, C. Chivigny, and others of the master furniture makers of the 18th century are among the craftsmen represented in the Burge "Signed Collection."

Unlike ordinary reproductions, Burge items have many handcrafted operations, and their quality can be seen in the finishing. He does not believe in chain and nail "beating up" of furniture to cause it to look old. Rather, his distressing simulates the furniture as it actually would look under aged condition, sometimes well-preserved as it might have been. Otherwise, it may have a less cared-for, but respected, finish—always authentic.

Moreover, these reproductions are not produced in unlimited quantities. Burge pieces are produced 12 to 24 at a time—24 being the very maximum.

VICTORIAN REPRODUCTIONS

Ascending the English throne in 1837, Queen Victoria reigned until 1901 and, during these delightful sixty-four years of her reign, a new style of furniture was born—Victorian. From the standpoint of sheer quantity, an enormous amount of furniture was produced. The population was growing and, with the rise of the prosperous middle class, there was an enormous demand for furniture. Because the demand exceeded the supply that cabinet makers could produce, furniture began to be machine-carved and mass-produced for the first time in the history of our country. Victorians had a proper respect for fine woods, so most of this furniture was sturdy and dignified, made of mahogany, black walnut or rosewood. These pieces were often uncomfortable, large, heavy, but always substantially built. Deep shades of upholstery, usually horsehair, and dark finishes made the pieces none too cheerful. Skillful combining of straight lines with curves from solid woods, with graceful carvings, consisting mostly of scrolls, leaves, classical figures, and flowers—flowers being predominant—gave quaint charm to many of the Victorian pieces. Pleasing to the eyes, these favorite motifs decorated the frames of the round, oval and oblong marble top occasional tables. During this era mirrors, like marble tops, decorated every possible piece.

Not all Victorian furniture is alike. Actually eight distinct styles were developed during this span of years and they are: Early or Transitional Victorian 1830's-1850; Victorian Gothic 1840-

1850's; Victorian Rococo (Louis XV) 1845-1860's; Spool Turned (Cottage) 1850-1880; Victorian Renaissance 1855-1875; Victorian Louis XVI 1865-1875; Eastlake (Jacobean) 1870's; and Turkish 1870-1880.

There is a revival of interest in Victorian furniture today, and many of the elegant old examples being hauled out of storage can lay claim to the status of antique. To supply the demand for Victorian pieces, marble-topped tables, sofas, side chairs and arm chairs are being reproduced. These new pieces, usually made of mahogany, are easily recognized because they look new and, to a knowing eye, the details are not always accurate.

Today the Victorian furniture manufacturing center of our nation is located at Montgomery, Alabama. Almost the entire business of manufacturing Victorian pieces has developed as an outgrowth of the Carlton McLendon Furniture Company. This industry, consisting of six factories, now produces 95 percent of the Victorian furniture made in the United States. All of the factories are located within one mile of the McLendon Company.

WILLIAMSBURG FURNITURE REPRODUCTIONS

All Williamsburg Furniture Reproductions are approved copies of eighteenth-century antiques in the restored buildings of Colonial Williamsburg, Williamsburg, Virginia. These pieces are known the world over for their distinction and unquestioned authenticity. Every reproduction is an exact replica of its antique prototype.

Williamsburg Furniture Adaptations were inspired by the handsome antiques in the restored buildings of Colonial Williamsburg. Whereas reproductions are always exact replicas of antiques, adaptations are made by modern construction methods, and when desirable in some cases they are redesigned for modern comfort, thus simplified in line and style. Williamsburg adaptations combine the traditional charm of eighteenth-century design with the ease of twentieth-century living. Carefully and thoughtfully, these adaptations are modified in varied ways to combine the best of the traditional style with the best of contemporary design. The result is a line of unusual furniture, graced with the fine proportions and details of the best antiques, and eminently suited to the graciousness of today's most distinguished homes.

The Williamsburg Hallmark is a combination of old and new symbols. The letter "C" and "W"

stand for Colonial Williamsburg, the educational organization financed by the late John D. Rockefeller, Jr., and responsible for the restoration of the colonial capital of Virginia. The elongated "4" ending in a double "X" has been called the "mysterious mark" because of the many and varied stories of its origin. It appeared in seventeenth- and eighteenth-century Virginia as a shipper's or maker's mark, often combined with the initials of planters and merchants. Even earlier it had been used in England in combination with watermarks and merchants' trademarks and signs. Today this mark has been combined with Colonial Williamsburg's initials to form the Williamsburg Hallmark, a registered trademark which is branded on their reproductions as well as adaptations.

HITCHCOCK CHAIR

Lambert Hitchcock of Hitchcocks-ville, Connecticut, is considered to be America's most famous chairmaker. His factory began operation in 1825, in the three-story brick factory which stands to this day. The high arrow weather vane on the cupola was the most distinctive sight in the settlement, which became known as Hitchcocks-ville.

The first chairs Lambert Hitchcock made had rush seats, but later ones were made with cane and solid wooden seats. These were marked "L. Hitchcock, Hitchcocks-ville, Connecticut, Warranted."

The basic woodworking style of all the production was the same, yet a considerable variety of the designs existed within it. The most popular top sections were the "pillow" and "bolster," but the "crown-top" and "roll-top" rails were also well known. Hitchcock also made Boston rockers, cradle settees or mammy benches, bureaus, tables, secretaries and stands. And it has been said that Hitchcock was one of the first to produce rocking chairs in a factory.

Chairs were assembled in the factory, as well as in homes of employees. Men did all the woodworking; the children rubbed on a priming coat of paint (always red).

Women did most of the decorating. They striped fine lines with quills, brushed gold bands on the front of the legs, cut stencil designs out of the best available paper, and laid them on tacky surfaces in sequence. With bare fingers or a piece of velvet, they rubbed the varicolored powders through the open stencil patterns and, finally, the finished product was then varnished.

In 1829 Hitchcock was forced into bankruptcy; however, his financial problems were quickly solved by Arba Alford, Jr., who became a partner in the firm. Chairs were then labeled "Hitchcock, Alford & Co., Hitchcocks-ville, Conn. Warranted." It is interesting to note that three "N's" on this mark were sometimes backward, and the cost prices for these chairs ranged from about 40 cents for the kitchen varieties to as much as $3.00 for the more elegant, rush-seated chairs.

Around 1843 Lambert Hitchcock left the company to establish another factory in Unionville, Connecticut, and the label on the chairs produced here read, "Lambert Hitchcock, Unionville, Connecticut."

On April 3, 1852, Lambert Hitchcock died suddenly at his home in Unionville and was buried in the nearby Riverside Cemetery in Farmington.

In 1946 John T. Kenney, with the late Richard E. Coombs, formed The Hitchcock Chair Company. Their purpose was to restore the original factory built by Lambert Hitchcock in 1826 and build additions to it for the reproduction of the chairs and cabinet furniture which made Hitchcocks-ville famous. Today the Chair Company is once again a vital part of the community, and the chairs produced here are marked with the stencil signature first used by the factory, but the "N" is cut backward as it was on the early chairs. Each new chair is also branded with the letters "H. C. Co."— under the front seat.

Today the word "Hitchcock" is a generic term, used by several different furniture manufacturers, though no other firm can use The Hitchcock Chair Company's trademark.

SHAKER FURNITURE

Shaker furniture is almost impossible to buy —and what there is reposes in museums or in jealously guarded personal collections. Until recently, no reproductions of Shaker furniture existed (except for chairs made at the Shaker Museum in Hancock, Massachusetts). Today, however, a number of pieces are being made in Spring Lake, Michigan, by an organization called the Guild of Shaker Crafts. And every piece is faithfully copied, and retains the marvellously gained proportions of the originals. The furniture is made of pine, and has a quite glossy natural finish that should improve as it mellows and loses some of its shine.

A religious sect, the Shakers migrated to this country from England in 1774. Their frugal philosophy disdained all ornament, and Shaker craftsmen made furniture of extraordinary simplicity and grace. It is the pursuit of perfection by which they are animated that gives their pieces power, and invests their simple forms with beauty. But it may be that Shaker furniture— "religion in wood," as an authority has styled it— is too intimately connected with Shaker beliefs to ever lend itself to reproductions by Non-Believers.

COHASSET COLONIALS

Original in
Henry Ford
Museum
WRITING
TABLE

Original in
Harrison Gray
Otis House
SIDE CHAIR

CHILD'S CHAIR
Original in
Wadsworth
Atheneum,
Hartford

Original in
Metropolitan
Museum
of Art

Cohasset Colonials
original
in
WADSWORTH ATHENEUM
by
HAGERTY
Cohasset, Massachusetts

Furniture made by Hagerty is
branded with this mark.

THE ILLUSTRATED "EXPANDED JOINT" AND "WEDGE JOINT" ALSO IDENTI-
FIES HAGERTY PIECES.

The Expanded Joint: Legs are assembled
in chair seats as shown. The tenon has
been compressed and, on contact with
glue, will swell filling the hole. This
swelling action results in a truly "welded"
joint.

This illustrates the Wedge joint.

144

PLANT STANDS, HAT RACKS, WHATNOTS

OAK TWIST FERN STAND, 36″ high, finished only.
OAK TWIST HAT RACK, 71″ high, finished or unfinished.
OAK BENTWOOD HAT RACK, 68″ high, finished or unfinished.
OAK TWIST FERN STAND, 24″ high, finished only.
BENTWOOD WALL RACK, three-prong, 22″ wide, finished only.
BENTWOOD WALL RACK (not pictured), four-prong, 30″ wide, finished only.
CORNER WHATNOT STAND, 53″ high, finished only.
BRASS HAT RACK, 72″ high, finished only.
STRAIGHT WHATNOT STAND, 54″ high, finished only.
COPPER MAGAZINE HOD, 15″ high.
BENTWOOD HAT RACK, four legs, 72″ high, finished only.
BENTWOOD HAT RACK, three legs, 73″ high, finished only.
PINE PLANT STAND, 36″ high, finished or unfinished.
PINE PLANT STAND, 31″ high, finished or unfinished.
PINE PLANT STAND, 26″ high, finished or unfinished.

(A-America, Inc.)

HITCHCOCK

The HITCHCOCK CHAIR Co.
RIVERTON (HITCHCOCKS-VILLE) CONN.

L. HITCHCOCK. HITCHCOCKS-VILLE. CONN. WARRANTED. ⊚

A registered trademark of The Hitchcock Chair Company

HITCHCOCK. ALFORD. & Co HITCHCOCKS-VILLE. CONN. ⊚
WARRANTED.

A registered trademark of The Hitchcock Chair Company

THE HITCHCOCK CHAIR COMPANY
Riverton (Hitchcocks-ville) Connecticut

MARKS WHICH HAVE IDENTIFIED "HITCHCOCK" CHAIRS

Hitchcock Chair—stenciled on rear seat rail "L. Hitchcock, Hitchcockville, Conn. Warrented." 1825-1828-maple and hickory painted black and stenciled. Courtesy of The Henry Ford Museum, Dearborn, Michigan.

The antique rocking chair on the left was made by Lambert Hitchcock in Hitchcocks-ville about 1828. Its recreation was made by The Hitchcock Chair Company at Riverton (formerly Hitchcocks-ville) in 1965.

Reproduced "Slatback" Chair
The Hitchcock Chair Company
Riverton (Hitchcocks-ville) Connecticut

Reproduced Side Chair
The Hitchcock Chair Company
Riverton (Hitchcocks-ville) Connecticut

146

FURNITURE AND LAMPS

BRASS HANGING OIL LAMP, three-way, etched glass.
CHERUB TABLE LAMP, 14″.
BRASS HANGING OIL LAMP, 10″.
BRASS HANGING OIL LAMP, 14″.
OAK LADY'S DESK W/DRAWER, 42″ high, finished or unfinished.
OAK STACK BOOKCASE, four tiers, 59″ high, finished or unfinished.
OAK CHAIR, double pressback, available W/arms, unfinished or finished.
OAK CHAIR, single pressback, finished or unfinished.
OAK CHAIR, double pressback, finished or unfinished.
OAK BALL and CLAW TABLES, 48″ W/24″ leaf; 36″ W/12″ leaf; 42″ W/18″ leaf; 54″ W/24″ leaf; finished or unfinished.
OAK LION'S HEAD TABLES, 48″ W/24″ leaf, 54″ W/24″ leaf, finished or unfinished.

(A-America, Inc.)

GOLD PAN OIL LAMP
OAK TOWEL BAR MEDICINE CHEST, beveled glass, two shelves, 25″ high, finished or unfinished.
OAK MEDICINE CHEST, stained glass, diamond mirror or beveled mirror, 30″ high, finished or unfinished.
OAK CHINA HUTCH, leaded glass doors, 78″ high, finished or unfinished.
OAK DINING TABLE W/four 12″ leaves, 42″ square, 30″ high, finished or unfinished.
OAK HAND MIRROR, finished only.
OAK TOILET SEAT, brass fittings, standard size, finished only.
CURTIS INDIAN PRINT, 13″, assorted.

TIFFANY SHADES AND BASES

SHADE and Tree base.
SHADE and Lily Pad base.
SHADE.
VICTORIAN BASE.
SHADE and Pompay base.
SHADE and Lion's Head base.
DESK LAMP.
SHADE and Tree Vine base.
FLORENTINE BASE.

SHADE.
SHADE and base.
SHADE.
MILAN BASE.
SHADE and square Gothic base.
SHADE.
DESK LAMP, inside-painted shade or etched glass shade.

(A-America, Inc.)

FURNITURE AND ACCESSORIES

OAK HALL TREE, 73″ high, finished or unfinished.

OAK OVAL MIRROR, 22″ x 36″, finished only.

CURIO CABINET, flat glass, 28″ high, finished only.

OAK CORNER CHINA, curved glass, 61″ high, finished or unfinished.

OAK BEVELED CHEVEL MIRROR, 68″ high, finished or unfinished.

OAK MIRROR (not pictured), not beveled, 68″ high, finished or unfinished.

PIANO STOOL, adjustable 19″ high, finished only.

PIANO STOOL, W/back, adjustable, 35″ high, finished only.

OAK ICEBOX, raised panels, deluxe hardware, 40″ high, finished or unfinished.

OAK COCKTAIL TABLE, 28″ high, finished or unfinished.

PUB TABLE, marble top, 26″ high.

L-1 LAMP, 16″ high.

L-2 LAMP, three-way, 21″ high.

L-3 LAMP, three-way, 25″ high.

(A-America, Inc.)

OAK SCHOOLHOUSE CLOCKS

(Left to Right)
OCTAGON CLOCK, 23″ high.
OCTAGON CLOCK, W/Ring, 28″ high.
OCTAGON CLOCK, 28″ high.
DELUXE CLOCK, 56″ high.
CARVED ROUND CLOCK, 28″ high.
ROUND CLOCK, 28″ high.
ROUND CLOCK, 23″ high.
(All with Ansonia-style movements.)

ROCKERS

(Left to Right)
DOUBLE PRESSBACK, sock bar and cane seat, 40″ high, finished or unfinished.
SINGLE PRESSBACK, cane seat, 38″ high, finished or unfinished.
THICK SEAT W/floral carved headrest, 47″ high, finished or unfinished.
CARVED BACK W/wood seat, 46″ high, finished or unfinished.
(Available Assembled or Knocked Down)

(A-America, Inc.)

FURNITURE

OAK CURVED GLASS CHINA, mirror back, glass shelves, 63″ high, finished or unfinished.
OAK MUST MIRROR, 38″ high, finished or unfinished.
BRASS WALL RACK, four-prong, 37″ wide.
OAK PARLOR DESK W/DRAWER, 50″ high, finished or unfinished.
OAK SECRETARY, side-by-side W/curved glass, 65″ high, finished or unfinished.
OAK WINDSOR CHAIR, finished or unfinished.
BRASS TOWEL BAR, 33″ high.
MINI CURVED-GLASS CURIO CABINET, 23″ high, finished only.
FOLDING TAPESTRY ROCKER, 32″ high.
FOLDING CANE ROCKER, 32″ high.
OAK SALOON CHAIR, carved rose press, finished or unfinished.
OAK OFFICE CHAIR, carved rose press, finished or unfinished.
COPPER OR BRASS DUTCH COAL HODS, set of five.

(A-America, Inc.)

NEW SHAKER FURNITURE

SHAKER OCTAGONAL CHEESE BOARD
(Original from dairy at Hancock, Mass., community.) Cleats on two ends. Pine and Oiled finish.

Rimmed Serving Tray (cherry) Used in communal dining room.

DOUBLE CUPBOARD
Courtesy of Guild of Shaker Crafts, Inc., Spring Lake, Michigan.

SHAKER COMMUNITY DINING TABLE (pine)
The trestle table has a pine board top and maple uprights and shoes. Edges of the posts chamfered.

SHAKER OVAL BOXES (new)
Courtesy of Guild of Shaker Crafts, Inc., Spring Lake, Mich. (Oval boxes were made by the Believers as early as 1798 for their own use. Later they were sold to the "world" in "nests" of 11 and 13. Made in natural finish or Shaker colors—Red, Heavenly blue, Ministry green, Meeting House blue, burnt orange, saffron.

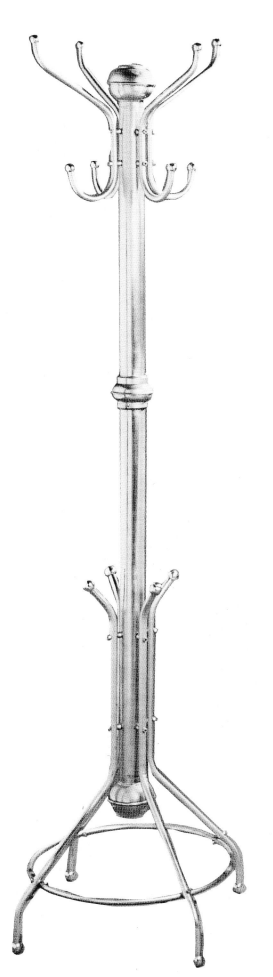

BRASS EXECUTIVE HAT RACK, 26″ high. (A. A. Importing Co., Inc.)

BRASS PLANT STAND, solid marble, top, 10¾″ square, 34″ high. (A. A. Importing Co., Inc.)

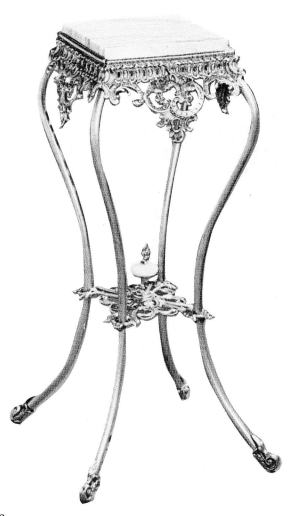

VICTORIAN BENTWOOD HAT RACK, 74″ high. (A. A. Importing Co., Inc.)

PRESS-BACK KITCHEN CHAIR. (A. A. Importing Co., Inc.)

"VICTORIAN" SHAVING STAND with rotating mirror, swivel candle-stick arms and movable gallery. Height adjustment from 52 to 60 inches. (A. A. Importing Co., Inc.)

TOWEL RAIL, 34½" high, 26½" across. (A. A. Importing Co., Inc.)

SWINGING CRADLE, 69" high, 48" across. (A. A. Importing Co., Inc.)

MASTER SPINNING WHEEL 26" across. (A. A. Importing Co., Inc.)

155

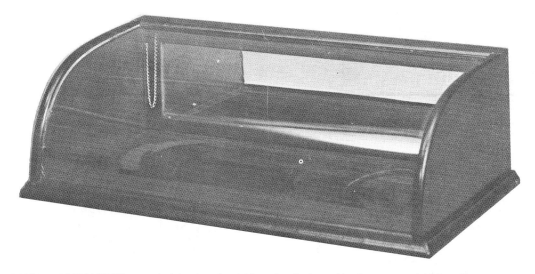

VICTORIAN CANDY CASE, curved, plate-glass front, hinged and mirrored back entry panel, lock and key, 32″ across. (A. A. Importing Co., Inc.)

VICTORIAN BUTTON-LEG ROUND TABLE, 29¾″ across, 28″ high. (A. A. Importing Co., Inc.)

VICTORIAN MARBLE-TOP OVAL TABLE, 34¼″ across, 26″ high. (A. A. Importing Co., Inc.)

WOODEN CORNER WHATNOT SHELF, mirrored back panels, 27¾″ high. (A. A. Importing Co., Inc.)

WOODEN MASTER SPICE CABINET, drawers with metal spice tags, side shelves for seasoning shakers, 16¼″ tall. (A. A. Importing Co., Inc.)

WOODEN MIRROR PLANTER-SCONCE, 23″ high, (A. A. Importing Co., Inc.)

WOODEN SWIVEL DRESSING MIRROR, mirror rotates, 15″ high. (A. A. Importing Co., Inc.)

BARONIAL WALL CLOCK, beveled side mirrors, four display shelves, lion-head crests, wooden case, key-wind, hour and half-hour chimes, 46″ high, 27″ wide. (A. A. Importing Co., Inc.)

CALENDAR "SCHOOLHOUSE" CLOCK, wooden case, 31-day key wind, hour and half-hour chimes, antique ivory face, brass pendulum, indicates date of month, 24″ high. (A. A. Importing Co. Inc.)

SARATOGA WALL CLOCK, wooden case, 31-day key wind, hour and half-hour chimes, pendulum and key, 26″ high. (A. A. Importing Co., Inc.)

VICTORIA SALON CLOCK, wooden case, 31-day key wind, hour and half-hour chimes, pendulum and key, 24″ high. (A. A. Importing Co., Inc.)

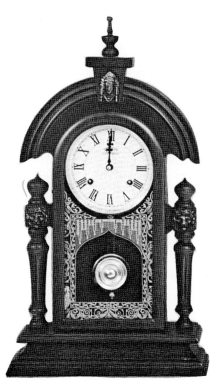

KING ARC-TOP CLOCK, wooden case, 31-day key wind, hour and half-hour chimes, pendulum and key, 24″ high. (A. A. Importing Co., Inc.)

"OPEN-CROWN" CLOCK, wooden case, 31-day key wind, hour and half-hour chimes, "draped-flags" gold pattern, antique ivory face, brass pendulum, 22″ high. (A. A. Importing Co., Inc.)

159

"RHEINLANDER" REGULATOR CLOCK, antique ivory face, R/A pendulum, lion head on crown, chime rods, 35¼" high. (A. A. Importing Co., Inc.)

"VIENNA" REGULATOR CLOCK, antique ivory face, R/A pendulum, "queen" head on crown, "bim-bam" gong, 35¼" high. (A. A. Importing Co., Inc.)

"BLACK FOREST" REGULATOR CLOCK, antique ivory face, R/A pendulum, "queen" head on crown, chime rods, 37½" high. (A. A. Importing Co., Inc.)

"LIBRARY" FREE-SWINGER CLOCK, antique ivory face, "lion" crest, brass pendulum bob, 38½" high. (A. A. Importing Co., Inc.)

"BERLINER" FREE-SWINGER CLOCK, "queen" crest, brass-finished face, brass pendulum bob, 37¾" high. (A. A. Importing Co., Inc.)

"GENERAL STORE" CLOCK, calendar dating, 32″ high. (A. A. Importing Co., Inc.)

Chapter IX
CAST IRON BANKS and TOYS

BANKS

Toy banks are properly divided into three classes: mechanical banks, still banks, and registering banks. Mechanical banks are banks in which some movement occurs when a coin is deposited. Still banks merely retain coins, and have no moving parts. These were made in an almost limitless range of materials. However, the reproduced banks being made today are of cast iron. Registering banks were made like cash registers, automatically adding up the sum of coins deposited. These are of more recent origin and, if they have been reproduced, they are unknown to me at this time.

Shortly after the Civil War, the first cast iron, mechanical "Penny" banks were manufactured. Here the mechanism was primed with a penny—a lever pushed, and the action began. They soon became the most popular savings toys ever to delight and enrich American children. These banks continued to be produced until the early 1900's, portraying many facets of life and customs.

Interest in mechanical banks has mushroomed during the last decade, with men in particular being attracted by them. Because of their popularity, many have been reproduced from originals. The first recast mechanical banks to appear on the market are easily identified, since the parts are heavier and fit together poorly, and the paint is pebbly instead of smooth. The surface or patina of aged paint has a smoothness in the touch and an appearance of age that cannot be duplicated artificially. New paint simply cannot be made to look old by wearing off portions of it, or by chipping it. Burning has become the latest method of aging, as well as a treatment with acid. Whenever the latter method is used, it leaves the surface of the bank very rough and pitted. The easiest way to determine whether a mechanical bank or a still bank is old is to examine the inside. The surface of an old bank has an appearance of age (resembles pewter), and is much smoother than the new interiors, due to the method used in making them. The interiors of the new banks are bright (resembling polished silver), and pebbly.

Still banks were made in an almost limitless range of materials. As prices rose on mechanical banks, still banks became popular with collectors, creating a demand for far more of the objects than could be supplied, hence reproductions were made of cast iron. When these banks have been artificially aged, they are difficult to authenticate—they are not marked.

The mechanical banks shown in this chapter have been reproduced from originals in the collection of *The Book of Knowledge*. Each new bank is marked on the base in raised letters "reproduced from original in collection of THE BOOK OF KNOWLEDGE," and many of the banks bear the original patent date. These new banks are showing up (especially at country auctions) with only the patent date on the bottom. The remaining words have been carefully removed, and the base smeared with paint to cover the file marks. In one instance, I noted that fine dirt and sand had been mixed with the paint—it chipped easily when scratched, revealing two flattened letters "D & G."

LIST AND DESCRIPTION OF MECHANICAL BANKS reproduced today by John Wright, Inc., Wrightsville, Pennsylvania. When a date follows the name of a bank, it indicates the year the original bank was produced.

CAST IRON TOYS

A variety of cast iron toys were made during the last half of nineteenth century. An extensive line produced in the 1880's included pull toy locomotives and numerous horse drawn vehicles. Surprisingly enough, the iron toy production continued into the early 1940's.

Because cast iron toys have become so popular and expensive in the antique field today, several firms have started making reproductions. It is very difficult to distinguish one of the new toys from an older one, if it has had any usage or has been artificially aged. Some of the early manufacturers of these toys marked their products, which has been helpful to collectors. If any of the reproduced toys are marked, I am not aware of it.

MECHANICAL BANKS

KICKING COW BANK (1888)
In this example a little boy sits placidly milking the cow. Suddenly bossy flips her tail, kicking over the boy and pail, and your coin is now safely inside the cow.

BUCKING BUFFALO BANK (1888)
With his big shaggy head the buffalo boosts the little boy toward the top of the stump. The racoon on the top draws back to hide and your coin falls into the base.

UNCLE REMUS (1890)
Uncle Remus stands in the doorway of a chicken house. He is carrying a sack of stolen chickens. When the head of the chicken (in the yard) is pressed, the policeman starts after the criminal, who darts back into the house —cornered.

INDIAN AND BEAR BANK (1888)
This mechanical bank has been the delight of antique coin bank collectors and small boys since it was first produced. The Indian warrior, in full regalia, shoots a coin into the menacing bear—and the bear snaps at the hunter.

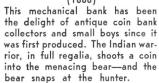

BOY ON TRAPEZE BANK
Just drop a coin in the boy's cap and he "Skins the cat" on the horizontal bar, depositing the coin in the ornate base.

HUMPTY DUMPTY BANK (1882)
To this clown, nothing tastes better than money! When a penny is placed in his hand, he pops it up to his mouth, sticks out his tongue, rolls his eyes blissfully heavenward, and swallows it.

MECHANICAL BANKS

KICKING MULE BANK (1879)

The "kicking mule bank" amused grandad when it was first produced long ago. The coin is placed in the jockey's mouth, a lever is pressed, the mule kicks, and the jockey flies over his head and deposits the coin in a slot in the bank's base.

DENTISTS BANK (1880)

Here all sorts of action takes place. The dentist's fee (a coin) is placed in his pocket. The tooth is extracted and both patient and dentist go sprawling. The coin drops from the dentist's pocket into a slot at the bank's base.

LEAP-FROG BANK (1891)

This mechanical bank is very realistic. When the coin is placed in the slot on top of the tree trunk, the action begins. The rear boy leap-frogs the other and hits a lever which dumps the coin in the tree.

ARTILLERY BANK (1877)

When the gun is loaded with a penny, draw back the hammer and the gunner raises his arm. The next step is to press the lever, and the gun roars as the gunner drops his arm, and your penny flies into the fort.

OWL BANK (1880)

The wise old owl turns his head to look at the penny that has been placed on the tree stump and, as he turns, the coin drops with a clink into the base. This example has very realistic glass eyes, and is 7¼ inches high.

TAMMANY (1873)

Notorious Boss Tweed is fat and greedy. If a coin is placed in his hand, he puts it in his pocket, nodding his thanks.

TRICK PONY (1885)

In this example the coin is placed in the pony's mouth. A lever in back of the base is pulled, the pony arches his neck, nods his head and deposits the coin in the manager.

ALWAYS DID 'SPISE A MULE BANK (1879)

This is a complicated bank, with a complicated name; however its action is a joy to behold. When a coin is placed beneath the little boy, the mule then spins around and kicks the poor lad over.

HOMETOWN BATTERY BANK (1888)

This charming example of 19th century craftsmanship depicts our national pastime as played in the 1880's. It's mechanical action is amazing. The pitcher throws the ball (coin), the batter swings and misses—and the coin i. caught by the catcher. All the action is fast, realistic and funny.

MAGICIAN BANK (1882)

The life-like figure of the magician stands behind a table. When a coin is placed on the table, the magician lowers his hat and nods his head. Then he raises his hat and lo! the coin has disappeared! into the bank, of course.

JONAH AND THE WHALE (1890)

There are 23 separate iron castings in this bank. The wobbly-jawed whale is apparently ready to swallow Jonah, who is being tossed at him by the boatman; however, he finally settles for the coin instead. The coin is placed on top of Jonahs headdress before the lever is pressed.

BULL DOG BANK

When a coin is balanced on the bull dog's nose, press his tail, and snap goes his jaw as he gobbles up the coin. The dog's head, jaw, and tail are movable, and he has very realistic glass eyes. This example is 7½ inches high.

MECHANICAL BANKS

WILLIAM TELL BANK
(1896)
This is one of the best known of all the mechanicals. Father William loads his gun with a coin, shoots the apple from his son's head and rings a bell inside the castle. All the action is started by pressing his right foot.

PUNCH AND JUDY (1882)
Here the coin is placed in Judy's dust pan—and the lever is pressed. Punch rushes at Judy, brandishing his club. Whack! Too late—Judy has already deposited the coin.

ORGAN BANK (1882)
Put a penny on the monkey's tray and turn the crank. Bells chime and the children dance as the monkey deposits the coin and very politely tips his cap.

TEDDY AND THE BEAR
(1907)
When Teddy Roosevelt's gun is loaded with a coin, he lowers his head, takes aim, and shoots the coin into the tree stump. Up pops a big fierce bear.

CAT AND MOUSE BANK (1891)
The pussycat smiles from the front of this bank, and a mouse peeks over the top. When a coin is placed in front of the mouse, and a lever is pressed, an acrobatic cat stands on his head, performing with a mouse.

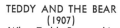

UNCLE SAM (1886)
When a coin is placed in Uncle's hand, press the button behind his umbrella. He waggles his whiskers while tossing the coin in a gapping carpet bag, which immediately snaps shut. In 1886, when this bank was originally produced, Uncle Sam made his collections with a smile.

MECHANICAL BANKS

CABIN BANK (1885)

Hands in his pockets, a trapper stands placidly in his cabin door, watching you place your coin on the roof. Move the handle of the white-wash brush, and he somersaults, heels over head, kicking your coin into his cabin through a slot in the roof.

EAGLE BANK (1883)

Place your coin in the eagle's bill. As her babies chirp, she leans over to feed them, flaps her wings, and deposits your coin in a slot in the nest.

PADDY AND THE PIG (1882)

When a coin is balanced on the pig's nose, he kicks it with his forefoot, flipping it toward his master. Paddy opens his mouth, sticks out his tongue to catch the coin, rolls his eyes upward and swallows it. This example was originally called "Shamrock Bank."

WORLD'S FAIR BANK (1892)

Here Columbus raises his arm and out of the ground rises an Indian. The coin rolls between the discoverer's feet into the bank. This bank commemorates the Columbian Exposition of 1892.

MECHANICAL BANKS

Original Eagle Bank
Courtesy of Mr. and Mrs. Chester Spreier

Reproduced Eagle Bank

Base of reproduced bank is on the right

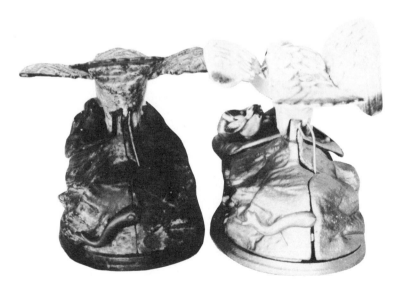

Reproduced bank on the right.
Note how poorly it fits together.

ROYAL ELEPHANT BANK
This majestic, colorful pachyderm takes
your coin in his trunk and, while swinging
his tail, deposits it in the royal seat on
his back.

U. S. CANNON (1898)
If you place a coin on the ship's turret, and load the cannon with
a marble, one shot brings down the ship's mast—and your coin
disappears into the hull.

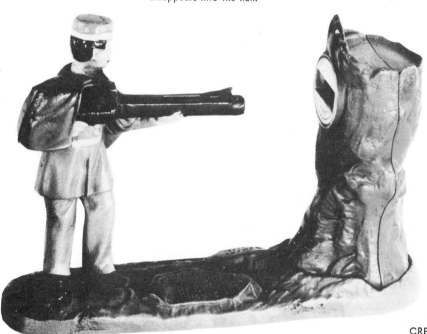

CREEDMORE BANK (1877)
When the soldier's gun is loaded with a coin, he shoots
it into the tree stump for a bull's eye. The soldier
sports an authentic 19th century uniform. This bank
is named for a famous old National Guard rifle range
on Long Island, New York.

CAST IRON STILL BANKS MADE BY
JOHN WRIGHT INC., WRIGHTSVILLE, PA.

Indian Head Bank

Santa Claus Bank

Merry-Go-Round Bank

Ice Cream Freezer Bank

Buffalo Bank

172

CAST IRON STILL BANKS MADE BY
JOHN WRIGHT INC., WRIGHTSVILLE, PA.

Pig

Cat

Hen

Fawn

Dog

Lion

Bull

CAST IRON STILL BANKS MADE BY
JOHN WRIGHT INC., WRIGHTSVILLE, PA.

Large Bull Dog Bank

Lucky Cabin Bank

St. Bernard Dog Bank

Sun Bonnet Sue Bank

Mail Box 4"

Treasure Chest 4"

Liberty Bell 4"

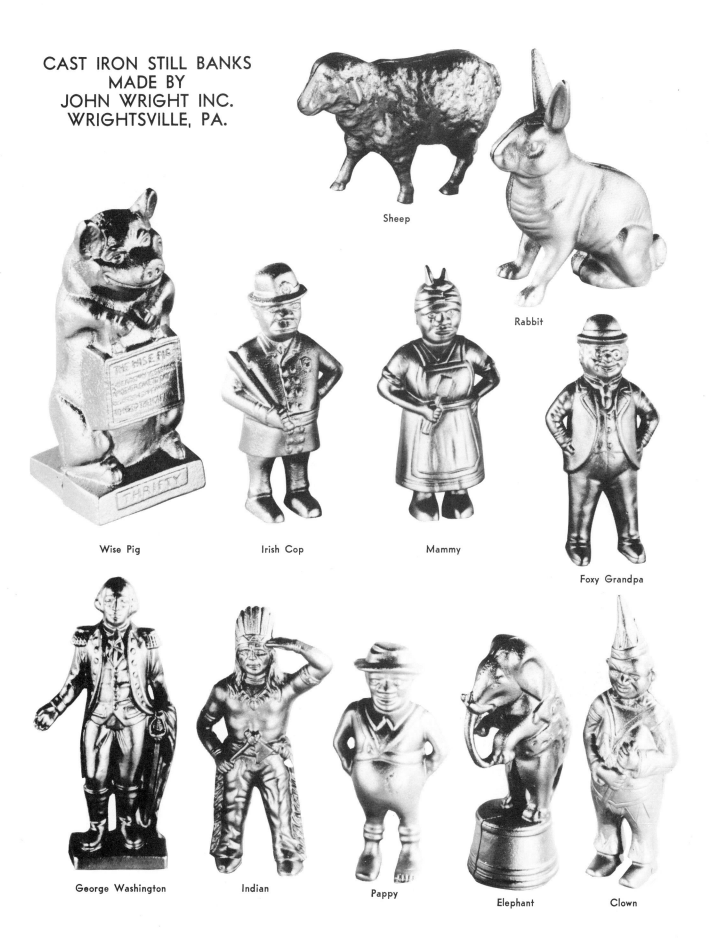

CAST IRON STILL BANKS
MADE BY
JOHN WRIGHT INC.
WRIGHTSVILLE, PA.

Sheep

Rabbit

Wise Pig

Irish Cop

Mammy

Foxy Grandpa

George Washington

Indian

Pappy

Elephant

Clown

175

CAST IRON STILL BANKS
MADE BY
JOHN WRIGHT INC.
WRIGHTSVILLE, PA.

Sheep Bank

Combination Safe Bank

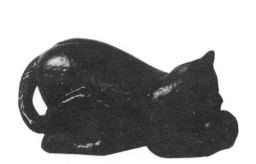

Cat Bank

Pony Bank

Rabbit Bank

Treasury Building Bank

Baby in Cradle Bank

Pig Bank

LOCOMOTIVE and TENDER—10" Long

FIRE ENGINE—10" Long

Cast Iron Toy

CAST IRON TOYS

ICE WAGON
Size 4½" x 9½"

LUMBER WAGON
11½" x 3" x 5¼"

STAGE COACH
11½" x 3" x 5"

HOOK AND LADDER ENGINE
15¼" x 3" x 5¼"

CAST IRON TOYS

AUTO
8" long

ENGINE PUMPER

ICE WAGON
10" x 2½" x 4½"

COVERED WAGON

Chapter X
METALWARE
and
WOODENWARE

METALWARE

The metal craftsman was very important to everyday living from Colonial days well into the nineteenth century. Almost anything could be made from one or more of the metals and, as a result, a vast number of essential articles were produced. There are many examples to be found in all parts of the United States and, however insignificant the article may be, it will be of interest to some collector, somewhere.

The shortage of good things has naturally brought reproductions on the scene—and some very authentic pieces are being made today in this field. The best guide in determining whether a piece is old or new is its condition. These pieces were made to be used just as often as we use our utensils today and, when a piece of pewter, copper, brass, etc., has been associated with life, it will retain the patina of years of usage and this surface appearance is impossible to reproduce.

Marks are also very helpful in the identification of old metalware, especially silver and pewter. Many silversmiths, as well as pewterers, marked their wares, and it is possible today to date most examples of their work, because there are several excellent reference books that picture the marks in detail.

Occasionally a good piece of pewter or silver is found with a bruised base where the "touch-mark" has been erased. When this has occurred, the area will be brighter.

METALWARE "LUCK AND WISDOM" NAPKIN RINGS, pair, 1¾". (A. A. Importing Co., Inc.)

METALWARE "BOY AND GIRL" NAPKIN RINGS, Pair, 1¾". (A. A. Importing Co., Inc.)

METALWARE "PUP AND KITTEN" NAPKIN RINGS, pair, 1¾". (A. A. Importing Co., Inc.)

THOMAS LOOSE METALWARE

The term "whitesmith" can be defined in two ways, one that works in white metal such as tin or steel, or one that finishes the rough product made by a blacksmith — using cold methods such as filing and hammering. Thomas Loose of Dauberville, Pa., does both the work of the blacksmith as well as the whitesmith exceedingly well.

Loose, a high school Industrial Arts instructor, began producing fine traditional forms in metal in 1970. Since that time he has designed and produced a variety of fine collectible items including latches and hinges, floor and table lamps, kettle and fat lamps, skewer sets, candleholders, forks, ladles, strainers, spatulas, spoons, hanging racks, revolving fireplace toasters, sewing birds, pie crimpers and various other tools.

In 1973, Loose began adding decorative touches to his products, and by 1976 had mastered the technique of inlaying brass by cutting out the area, then pouring molten brass into the space, cooling, filing, and polishing the metal and, finally, producing a perfect inlay. All items produced are marked "T LOOSE" and most are dated.

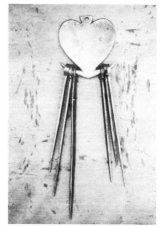

Skewer Set by Thomas Loose.

Heart-shaped Trivet with brass decoration by Thomas Loose.

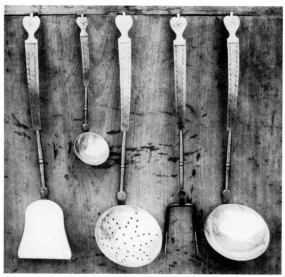

Steel and Brass Ladle, Fork, Skimmer Tasting Spoon and Spatula with intricate brass inlay by Thomas Loose.

182

BRASS

Early pieces of golden yellow brassware were used for a wide range of cooking utensils such as long-handled skimmers, forks, ladles (many with long iron handles), teakettles, etc. Each piece was the product of a craftsman, not a factory. Antiques made of brass are very sturdy and, generally, an early piece is in good condition when found.

It is not a difficult task to tell a modern coal scuttle (many are being produced with Delft handles), carriage lamp, or cooking utensil from an early example, as color is a true indication of age. Modern brass pieces will turn red when they become tarnished, whereas an early piece of brassware will never turn red when tarnished.

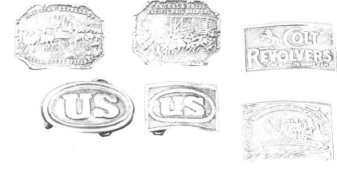

BRASS BUCKLES, "American Express," "Colt Revolvers," "US," etc., up to 3¾" across. (A. A. Importing Co., Inc.)

BRASS SHIP'S BELL, brass clapper, 9⅝" high. (A. A. Importing Co., Inc.)

BRASS "BEEHIVE" CANDLESTICKS, pair, 9⅝" high. (A. A. Importing Co., Inc.)

BRASS LADLE SET, iron handles, 5" to 6¾" across. (A. A. Importing Co., Inc.)

183

COPPER

Copper can be distinguished by its golden pink glow and, like brass, the early pieces were used essentially for utilitarian articles. During the late 1700's copper sheets were produced in America by hammering and, later, by rolling. Until that time they were imported. About 1800, American metalsmiths advertised copper kettles of all sizes, as well as coffee pots, saucepans, bedwarmers, pitchers, measures, etc.

Much copper is being reproduced today, including kitchen utensils of all sizes and descriptions. However, the appearance of the new examples is different from the early pieces, making identification easy for collectors. The new ware is light weight and shines brightly. Furthermore, it lacks dents, bruises and the inimitable patina old copper acquires through years of use.

IRON

Very interesting items have been produced from iron since the first iron works opened about 1650. However, there were few forges and furnaces until the turn of the eighteenth century, when many sprang up in the Northeast. Blacksmiths created a variety of essential things which included iron utensils, tools and farm implements. Practically all of the collectible ironware available today is nineteenth century pieces.

Ironwares are still being made in early shapes—many of which are confusing collectors, especially pieces that have been used for several years or have been cleverly aged to indicate years of usage. To tell the difference between a nineteenth-century trivet, still bank, toy, etc., and a twentieth-century reproduction often requires expertise to differentiate the slight variations. Therefore, I have illustrated numerous reproductions, because it is very important that collectors know what is currently being manufactured.

PEWTER

Pewter was more generally used than other metals for tableware and utensils from Colonial days until around 1850. It is an amalgam of base metals, chiefly tin and copper, plus varying amounts of other metals. Its color is determined by the variance of the chemical composition. Some pieces have an almost silver-like appearance, while other pieces are dull, pale bluish-gray. Pewter is softer than other metals; it can be scratched, dented, or bent very easily. It also corrodes and develops tiny pits. An old piece of early pewter

always feels slightly rough to the touch, and has a quite different color from the twentieth-century reproductions.

Early pieces of pewter usually carry a "touchmark" signifying the maker. American pewterers adopted individual touchmarks which were impressed on a finished piece in an inconspicuous place. It might be a name, two or more initials, or a series of symbols such as an eagle, dove, ship or rose. Names or initials of the maker were the usual marks of later pieces.

American pewter was simple and sturdy. Decoration was usually confined to beaded edges, and the pierced designs of porringer handles. Foreign examples were usually heavily embellished with decoration.

English craftsmen were subject to guild regulations which required their wares be stamped with hallmarks indicating the maker, his town, the year, the sterling quality of the metal and the reigning monarch.

SILVER

The manufacture of silverware in the United States began about 1842. It replaced pewter in the American home, just as pewter had earlier replaced woodenware. An aged piece of silver has a soft richness of color, combined with an unmistakable patina that is quite different from the bright new silver being produced today. Of all the collectibles in metalware, silver is in a class by itself and the pieces reflect the taste of their times. In order to avoid mistakes in this field, collectors must have some knowledge of style, workmanship, and decoration, as many pieces of nineteenth-century silver carry no mark.

The style of the lettering is always a clue to identifying new silver pieces. There are many excellent and acknowledged reproductions on the market today, such as the Williamsburg Reproductions and the Regal Reproductions illustrated in this chapter. These pieces are marked "C Co." for Corbell Company; their trademark which is a castle; and the letters "S.P." for silver plate. In addition, there are many cheap, unmarked pieces which have caused much confusion among collectors. They are: silver-plated caster frames with traditional 5-hole revolving tray; caster bottle tops, two-hole caster frame; pickle caster, ornate tongs, and a variety of souvenir spoons.

FIREMARKS

Firemarks date from the 1700's and were used until the mid-1800's, before the days of mechanized fire equipment. They were furnished to clients by insurance companies, and were fastened to the front of a building indicating to the volunteer fireman that the owner had paid for special fire protection. And therefore, a reward would be paid as the house or business building was worth saving.

Because these old firemarks seem to fascinate almost everyone, cast iron reproductions have been made. The original plaques or firemarks were made of wood, cast iron, lead or tin.

Reproduced Large Firemarks
Cast Iron
Hand Painted

Clasped Hands
Size 7½" x 11"

F. I. Engine Co.
Size 11¾" x 13¼"

Valiant Hose Decorated
Size 5¾" x 10½"

Tree
Size 7½" x 11"

Fireman
Size 8¾" x 11¼"

F & A Hose
Size 6¾" x 10¾"

Eagle Hose
Size 8¾" x 11"

U. F. FIREMAN
Size 11¼" x 8¾"

U.F.I.C. Decorated
Size 7½" x 10¾"

TRIVETS

Trivets were designed to keep hot pans, kettles and dishes either over the fire or close to it. The reason for three legs is because of the rough, uneven surface of the fireplace or hearth. A trivet with three legs will stand steady, whereas one with four legs requires a level, smooth surface to stand steady.

Early trivets were imaginatively hand wrought in a variety of designs, but by the middle of the nineteenth century, cast iron replaced wrought iron in the general manufacture of trivets. Trivets were also made of wood (rare), brass, copper, wire, silver and tin. The latter ones are actually thin sheet iron that has been tin plated.

A great number of trivets have been reproduced, many from original molds, making identification difficult in most instances. These new examples are being made from aluminum (lightweight), brass, white metal and iron. Some collectors believe that the early trivets made from the latter are thinner than the later ones, but this cannot always be considered a reliable test. However, any trivet with the name of the trivet on the back is modern and, interestingly enough, many of the new trivets have a number either raised or indented on the backside.

Other cast iron reproductions currently being manufactured are match holders, both the table and hang-on-the-wall type, and twine holders.

New cast iron trivets made by B. & P. LAMP SUPPLY CO.

TINWARE

Phil Kelly

The new tinware items shown here were produced by Phil Kelly, a contemporary Pennsylvania craftsman in the tradition of yesterday. Mr. Kelly's shop is located at the Pennsylvania Farm Museum, Landis Valley, Pa. Here, for more than a decade, he has produced a wide variety of outstanding tin objects. All items are marked.

Tinware by Phil Kelly and Elmer Smith, author of the book *Tinware*.

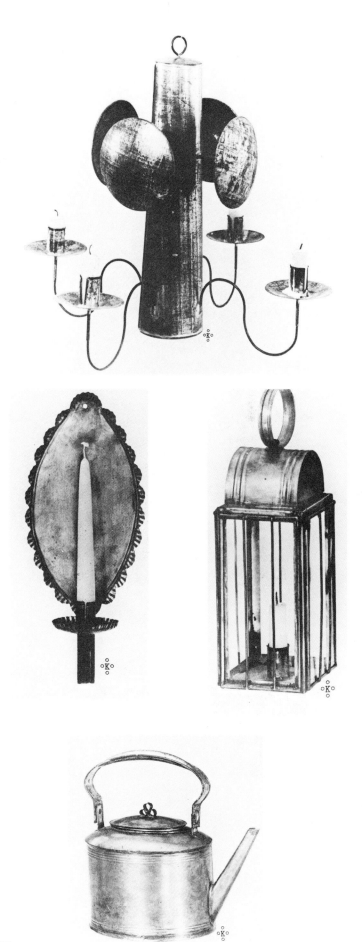

187

TINWARE

Hurley Patentee Items

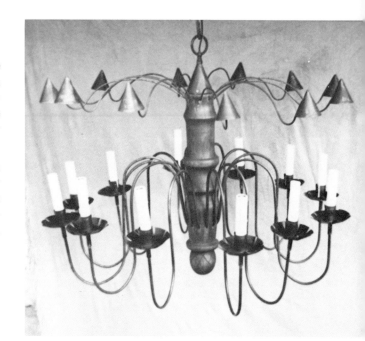

The sconces, lamps and chandeliers shown here have been reproduced as you would have purchased them 200 years ago. Each is a faithful copy of an outstanding seventeenth or eighteenth century piece. The originals of all Patentee lighting fixtures are presently in museums or private collections.

Each piece of wood or metal used in the production of Hurley Patentee items is handcrafted in the manner of the early days which the piece represents. This careful individual crafting gives each of their reproductions a very old appearance. All items produced by the firm are marked with the jointed letters "HP," (note illustration of trademark).

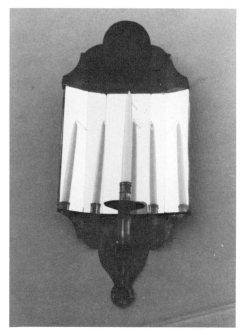

Handcrafted by Hurley Patentee Manor

PAUL REVERE LANTERNS

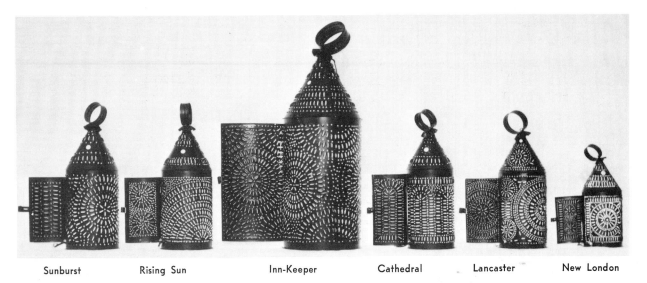

Sunburst   Rising Sun   Inn-Keeper   Cathedral   Lancaster   New London

The name "Paul Revere Lantern" has been long and widely used to designate the interesting and attractive pierced tin lanterns in common use during the American Colonial and Revolutionary days. Their American manufacture began about 1650, first of iron and later of tin.

Making pierced tin lanterns was a widely practiced European folk art, from which American craftsmen developed many variations. Among their favorite basic designs were the cathedral, the rising sun, and the sunburst, usually executed with skill and taste, and always with individual character peculiar to hand work. The lanterns vary in size; however, an average one is about 6 inches in diameter, and 14 inches high, not including the ring handle which is attached to the peak of the cone-shaped top.

Although the lanterns were made long before Paul Revere (1735-1818) was born, the persistent linking of these simple and appealing household articles with him implies some historical connection and, after Longfellow's stirring poem "Paul Revere's Ride" appeared in the *Atlantic Monthly* in 1861, the lanterns have borne his name.

Research into the signalling activities of that fateful night leads to considerable controversy. The Concord Antiquarian Society exhibits a "well-made glass-sided lantern" said to be one of those hung in the belfry of Christ (North) Church, popularly acknowledged as the signalling place. A considerable body of scholarship indicates, however, that the actual signal was sent from the Second Church, where Revere was a member of the governing board. A pierced tin lantern cannot be rejected, as some have tried, on the grounds that it would emit only a feeble light. With the door open and the bright tin interior serving as a reflector, this type of lantern actually throws a brighter beam than does one with glass sides.

Thus the inconclusive battle rages, but one thing remains sure: Paul Revere was a fine silversmith—and every American pierced tin lantern will always be known as a "Revere" lantern, although there is no record that the young craftsman ever made one.

Today faithful reproductions of the old pierced tin lanterns are being produced by the **Revere Lantern Shop, New London, Pennsylvania. These** examples, with their wrought iron black finish, have been reproduced from the most pleasing designs and, like the originals, their beauty, individuality and usefulness makes them particularly appealing to collectors.

The six patterns made by the Revere Lantern Shop are: Sunburst, Rising Sun, Inn-Keeper, Cathedral, Lancaster, and New London.

The Sunburst lantern is an authentic reproduction of an antique Pennsylvania Revere lantern. It is a simple circular pattern which casts a vigorous pattern of light on walls and ceilings, with its 650 pierced holes. Its height (to top of ring) is 15½ inches—diameter 5½ inches.

Rising Sun pattern is an exact copy of an antique New Hampshire Revere lantern. This is

An Original Pierced Tin Lantern

an unusually graceful pattern, with its 1,450 pierced holes. It throws a beautiful fan-shaped pattern of light on the wall. Its height is 15½ inches—diameter 5½ inches.

The Inn-Keeper pattern is a double sunburst pattern. Its large size makes it especially adaptable to large rooms. With a 75-watt clear bulb is projects a strong, sharp pattern of light on its surroundings. It has 1600 pierced holes, is 25 inches tall and its diameter is 8½ inches.

Cathedral pattern is a copy of an antique Revere lantern found in Boston. This was a popular pattern for the early lanterns, and its high arches create one of the most effective designs when used as a candle model. It has 1,150 pierced holes, its height is 14½ inches, and the diameter is 5 inches.

The Lancaster pattern is one of the most beautiful, and the original of this pattern came from Lancaster County, Pennsylvania. Its 2,050 pierced holes give it a lacy, intricate design. Its height is 14½ inches, and the diameter is 5 inches.

The New London pattern is only 11 inches high, and 4 inches in diameter. It is a double sunburst pattern, with 1,500 small pierced holes which give it a particularly delicate appearance.

These new pierced tin lanterns can be purchased with a candle holder, unwired without the candle holder, or electrified. They are made from terne plate, which is made by dipping a sheet of steel in a molten alloy of 20 percent tin and 80 percent lead. The early lanterns were made of sheet iron and, later, of tin. Since sheet iron rusts badly in the weather, or even from dampness indoors, many of the early lanterns rusted away long before they ever became antiques, and the lanterns which have survived the march of time probably date from the early nineteenth century.

Although some reproduced lanterns are being artificially aged, fortunately for the collector there are several ways of distinguishing the early lanterns from the new ones. Disregard and rough handling in the past has caused dents on the early lanterns, closing many of the numberless perforations through which the light shines. In addition, natural wear is especially noticeable around the rim of the cone-shaped top and lap-joined base. It is always wise to examine the rectangular door, the central candleholder and the interior of a pierced tin lantern before you buy, as these areas will show wear marks that indicate usage.

The perforations on the old lanterns feel dull to the touch, are irregular, and the surface of the lantern feels pebbly. The perforations on the new lanterns feel quite sharp, they are very regular, and the surface feels smooth when touched. The interior of the old lanterns is dull, discolored pebbly and scratched. But the interior of the reproduced examples is as bright and shiny as a new piece of silver. All of the artificially aged lanterns that I have seen have the usual dents here and there, but what really gives them away is their painted interiors, which cleverly covers the new shiny tin until it is scratched. So—if you will take the time to note carefully these differences between the old and the new, you will discover that it is not difficult to distinguish one from the other.

NEW HANDCRAFTED AND HAND DECORATED
EARLY AMERICAN TINWARE
Courtesy of Burkart Bros., Inc.

Pepper and Salt

Pitcher

Cheese Tray

Treasure Chest

Sconce

Tea Pot

Pitcher

TOLEWARE

The gayly-colored tinware of the Dutch country stems from a European background, in this instance Wales and Holland. Much of the ware was produced in Pennsylvania during the first half of the nineteenth century, and this group of utilitarian articles comes under the general classification of tole, or Pennsylvania Toleware. It was decorated with stenciling, as well as with freehand. The most popular designs included birds, flowers, fruits and geometric designs. The colors used were old pumpkin yellow, yellow ochre, cream, blue, white, green, black, brown and Indian red. The work was done in both colored bronze and oil paints.

Amazingly enough, much of the old undecorated tinware has been painted and decorated lately for the benefit of the unsuspecting collector, and some pieces look very convincing! However, the surface of a really old piece of toleware is almost always crisscrossed with a maze of tiny age checks on the background, as well as in the design. Additional clues indicating antiquity are chipped and faded paint, scratches and bruises.

Since 1966 a number of very beautiful and authentic pieces of new toleware has been produced in Verplanck, New York, by Burkart Brothers, Inc. Each handcrafted replica is carefully antiqued (with painted interior), decorated and signed by the artist. It is easy for collectors to recognize these pieces, because they look new.

"Yankee Peddler Toleware"
Courtesy of Burkart Bros., Inc., Verplanck, New York

WOODEN WARE

Wooden ware is also called treenware, from the name of its origin, the tree. It played a very important part in the homes of the 17th and 18th centuries in Colonial America, and was used in a variety of ways. There is a common and universal interest in practically all of these old, ordinary objects—they are treasured by collectors.

Wooden ware is still being made and sold. However, the majority of the new pieces are not being made to fool the collector; but, when weathered, stained or battered to simulate usage, plus a clever sales pitch made by an unscrupulous seller, numerous pieces are passed off each year as 18th and 19th century versions.

When comparing today's factory-made products with earlier pieces that were whittled by hand with a knife, or made with hand tools while being held on a lathe—there is a noticeable contrast. The early pieces show crude workmanship, cutting is uneven, and tool marks have been worn smooth. In addition, time brings lightness and a mellow appearance to aged wood. Actually, some of the early examples such as butter paddles, plates, small scoops, etc., are so lightweight that they seem almost hollow—and do have a hollow tone when tapped.

New wooden ware pieces causing the greatest confusion in the field are:

    Bowls in various sizes
    Boxes, oval in 13 different sizes
    Butter Churn (various sizes with metal hoops)
    Butter Molds, Prints and Paddles
    Dippers
    Knife Box
    Mortars with Pestles
    Plates, in two different sizes
    Potato Masher
    Rolling Pin
    Spoon Racks
    Sugar Bucket with metal hoops
    Tray
    Wooden Scoops in various sizes

WOODEN BUTTER MOLDS, plunger, case and six press-patterns; Pineapple, Swan, Bird-in-Tree, Wheat, Daisy and Flower, 5¼" high. (A. A. Importing Co., Inc.)

BOX BUTTER MOLDS, plunger, dovetailed case and six carved prints, 5¼" across. (A. A. Importing Co., Inc.)

WOODEN BUTTER PADDLES, (4), 20" long. (A. A. Importing Co., Inc.)

194

Chapter XI
MISCELLANEOUS

COFFEE MILLS

COFFEE MILL, walnut, side mill with black satin finish, adjusting screw at side of hopper, works lever at back of mill, hardwood board heavily varnished, 8½″ x 2″ x 6½″. (Conestoga Studios)

AMERICAN BEAUTY SIDE COFFEE MILL, lithographed three-color metal container on black satin iron grinder, wall mounted. (Conestoga Studios)

COFFEE MILL, iron parts, satin black finish; available in stained walnut or unfinished, 6″ x 6″ x 4″. (Conestoga Studios)

COFFEE MILL, iron top with grip handle, double lock-nut regulator, 6″ x 6″ x 5″. (Conestoga Studios)

COFFEE MILL, iron parts, satin black, double lock-nut regulator, adjustable grinder, 6¾″ x 6¾″ x 5⅛″. (Conestoga Studios)

WALNUT SPICE MILL, 4¼″ x 4¼″ x 3″. (Conestoga Studios)

DECOYS

Contemporary decoys creating the most stir among collectors are those carved by Percy L. Perkins of Seabrook, N.H. The retired shoe worker carves decoys of about fifteen different varieties of marsh birds as a hobby in a small workshop behind his mobile home. These carvings are actual decoys, ranging in size from small sandpipers to large ducks. The forms are carved out of white pine and mostly are carved from one piece of wood. Smaller birds, such as the Hudsonian and Labrador curlews, are carved from a solid chunk of pine, but the ducks are done in two pieces, a head portion and a body piece.

All work on the birds is done by hand. Perkins first step is to rough out the decoys with a hatchet and then hand-carve each piece with knives and sand until smooth. Some of the decoys are carved from timbers more than 200 years old. The eighty-year-old bird carver marks each of his decoys on the bottom with the letter "P", deeply carved into the wood.

Hand-carved shore birds by Percy L. Perkins.

DISNEY REPRODUCTIONS

As the result of recent interest in Disneyana, a number of new items have been produced to confuse the collector. These are:

1) Mickey Mouse post office bank, in the shape of a red post office box.
2) Round belt buckle with Mickey Mouse holding a pencil and reading "Mickey Mouse 1937 Hollywood Cal U.S.A." On the backside, the buckle is marked "Sun Rubber Co USA" or "Tiffany and Co., London, England." The Sun Rubber Company did not become a Disney licensee until 1941, and never produced metal belt buckles.
3) A rectangular belt buckle which features Minnie Mouse looking through a telescope.
4) Mickey Mouse cast iron bookends, featuring Mickey leaning against a book. These date from 1972, and were made by John Wright, Inc. of Wrightsville, Pa. — a manufacturer of reproductions, under license by Walt Disney Productions.
5) Mickey Mouse pocket mirror featuring an early Mickey Mouse Club illustration of "Chief Mickey Mouse" button.
6) Ingersoll clock featuring Mickey and Minnie Mouse kissing, unauthorized item that was never mass-produced.
7) Ingersoll Mickey Mouse pocket watch which has a longer copyright notice than the original example. Additionally, the backside is not debossed with the figure of Mickey Mouse.
8) A pinback button measuring 3½" in diameter and featuring both Mickey and Minnie at the piano, labelled "Yoo Hoo!" This item has a 1930 copyright printed on the rim, but has recently been made.
9) Cast iron Mickey Mouse flag holder and paperweight. This item was also made by John Wright, Inc. in 1972.

PAINTINGS ON WOOD

Once, painting on boards was commonplace, especially in the rural areas. Dorothy Davis, prominent Yarmouthport, Mass., folk artist, paints on old cutting boards of various sizes, giving her paintings a special nostalgic charm that appeals to all age groups. Her paintings are oftentimes mistaken for an eighteenth or nineteenth century work of art, because of the fine qulaity of her work and the aged wood on which the scenes are painted.

Painting on wood by Dorothy Davis

THEOREM PAINTING

The term "theorem" simply means routine or theoretical excerises in painting, done on velvet or paper (rare), with the aid of stencils. This was an artistic skill taught in fashionable young ladies' seminaries from about 1810-1845. Topics included still lifes, showing colorful baskets of fruit or flowers with an occasional bird or butterfly, in addition to portraits and landscapes.

David Y. Ellinger of Pottstown, Pennsylvania is considered to be one of the greatest theorem painters of our time. He grew up in the slowly changing, peaceful Dutch Country. Through his art flows the entire tradition of Pennsylvania Dutch culture which is his heritage. Ellinger is self-taught, and his creative talents rise fresh and pure without alien influence. Examples of his work are owned by many private collectors and museums throughout the country.

Another artist who has achieved success in this field is Marjorie S. Yoder of Morgantown, Pa. Yoder, a former English teacher with a M.A. degree in American Folk Culture, has been painting theorems for ten years. She also produces colorful fabric stenciling, in addition to wall and floor stenciling.

Painting by David Y. Ellinger

Painting by Marjorie S. Yoder

TRADITIONAL SCISSORS CUTTINGS

Scherenschnitte, or scissors cuttings in the Pennsylvania German tradition, are derived from the Swiss-German technique of cutting one piece of paper in a continuous design, even though the paper can be folded from one to three times, repeating the overall pattern.

Earliest forms coming to America in the late eighteenth century are found to be birth certificates and love letters. The art flourished in a variety of different forms until the early twentieth century when valentines, doilies, shelf paper, cards, cut-out books and the beautiful hand-made certificates became mass-produced.

During the last decade, Claudia Hopf of Womelsdorf, Pa. has revived the art of traditional paper cuttings. Today, examples of her colorful paper cuttings are owned by museums here and in Europe, and by many private collectors throughout the country. Her cuttings range from landscapes to fanciful valentines with intricate lacy borders. And by using a limited number of colors to decorate her cuttings, she achieves a very old appearing work of art. All examples are signed "C. HOPF."

For additional information, I suggest the book *Scherenschnitte, Traditional Papercutting* written and illustrated by Mrs. Hopf and published by Applied Arts Publishers, Lebanon, Pa.

Scissors cutting by Claudia Hopf

WOOD CARVINGS

The artistic ingenuity and inventive craftsmanship of the American woodcarvers have contributed greatly to our cultural history. Much of their work was quite primitive while other specimens were intricately carved and well-executed. Appreciation for the fanciful objects produced by these naive, non-academic, native artists and craftsmen has developed slowly over the years, to the extent that they are sought by private collectors and museums alike.

Best known to collectors of fine rural folk art are the works of the almost legendary, wandering whittler, Wilhelm Schimmel, who according to tradition, tramped throughout southeastern Pennsylvania for a period of about thirty years after the Civil War, carving toy figures and fierce-looking eagles in various sizes.

Nowadays, whether the object be a decorative carved bird or animal, a figure group, a weathervane — or something purely utilitarian — not necessarily old enough to qualify as an "antique," it is classified as an example of Folk Art.

Today, this tradition is being carried on by Daniel and Barbara Stawser in the village of Stouchsburg, Pa. Strawser's first attempts were close facsimiles of the Schimmel pieces. However, as he progressed his individualism emerged in the creation of his forms — developing a style and decoration that is unmistakably Strawser's. Although Strawser is best known for his bird trees, he also carves, and Barbara decorates, eagles in various sizes, plus additional detailed groupings such as Adam and Eve in the Garden of Eden — or Noah's Ark.

Contemporary hand-carved spoon rack 7½" W, 16¼" H.
(Will Noad)

Hand-carved and decorated eagle by Barbara and Daniel Strawser.

202

ABOUT THE AUTHOR

Dorothy Hammond, author, artist and columnist, is among the foremost authorities on the subject of antiques and reproductions. Her writing has taken various forms; she has written for both adults and children, and for eleven years has written the nationally-syndicated newspaper column "Antique Wise" for Columbia Features, Inc., of New York now appearing in over 170 papers.

Mrs. Hammond was motivated to write this book because of the many letters received daily from readers wanting to know whether an object is genuine or a reproduction. Realizing that the number of collectors has never been equaled in history, and that all fields of collecting have become saturated with confusing new objects, she felt that there was a need for a book of this type, because collectors should know what has been produced and what is currently being made, in order that they can accumulate meaningful collections — because prices are too high for speculation in the neglected field of confusing collectibles.

BIBLIOGRAPHY

Rainwater, Dorothy T. *American Silver Manufacturers.*

Godden, Geoffrey. *Encyclopedia of British Pottery & Porcelain Marks.*

Gould, Mary Earle. *Antique Tin & Tole Ware & Early American Wooden Ware.*

Ormsbee, Thomas H. *Field Guide to American Victorian Furniture, Field Guide to Early American Furniture,* and *Know Your Heirlooms.*

Coleman, Dorothy S., Elizabeth A., and Evelyn J. *The Collector's Encyclopedia of Dolls.*

Belknap, E. M. *Milk Glass.*

Kauffman, Henry J. *American Copper & Brass.*

Blount, Berniece and Henry. *French Cameo Glass.*

Robacker, Earl F. *Pennsylvania Dutch Stuff.*

Griffith, F. H. *Mechanical Bank Booklet.*

Hankenson, Dick. *Trivets.*

Hardt, Anton. *Souvenir Spoons of the 90's.*

Lee, Ruth Webb. *Antique Fakes and Reproductions, Nineteenth Century Art Glass,* and *Victorian Glass.*

Shull, Thelma. *Victorian Antiques.*

Hartung, Marion T. *Carnival Glass,* Books I-IV.

Revi, Albert Christian. *American Cut & Engraved Glass, American Pressed Glass and Figural Bottles* and *Nineteenth Century Glass.*

Winter, Herbert. *Tiffany Favrile Glass.*

McClintock, Marshall and Inez. *Toys in America.*

Barret, Richard Carter. *Identification of American Art Glass.*

Koch, Robert. *Louis C. Tiffany, Rebel in Glass.*

Jenkins, Dorothy H. *A Fortune in the Junk Pile.*

Kovel, Ralph and Terry. *Know Your Antiques*
    Dictionary of Marks, Pottery and Porcelain
    American Country Furniture
    Directory of American Silver, Pewter and Silver Plate

Cole, Ann Kilborn. *How to Collect the "New" Antiques.*

McClinton, Katherine Morrison. *A Handbook of Popular Antiques.*

Grover, Ray and Lee. *Art Glass Nouveau.*

INDEX